HVAC For Beginners

With Diagrams and Images - The Bible to Mastering Heating, Ventilation, and Air Conditioning Systems. Learn the Fundamentals, Installation Techniques, Maintenance Tips, and Energy-saving Strategies

BRAD LIPSEY

Table of Contents

I hope you enjoy the book! If you find any errors or want to provide feedback, please write to mbagencypress@gmail.com. Thank you

Book 1

Introduction to HVAC Systems

Understanding the Basics of Heating, Ventilation, and Air Conditioning

What is HVAC?

Heating, ventilation, and air conditioning, or HVAC, is a complete system utilized in residential, commercial, and industrial settings to create cozy and healthful indoor conditions. It includes a variety of tools, techniques, and ideas that come together to regulate a building's temperature, humidity, air quality, and airflow.

Figure 1.1 Air Curtain

The main goal of HVAC systems is to provide inhabitants with an ideal interior climate that will ensure their comfort and wellbeing. These systems are essential in ensuring that ideal conditions are maintained regardless of the weather outside, enabling people to live, work, and participate in activities in a controlled environment.

HVAC systems must have a heating component, especially in colder climates. In cold weather, it entails the process of increasing the indoor temperature to a comfortable level. Furnaces, boilers, and heat pumps are often used heating appliances. Boilers heat water to produce steam or hot water that is distributed throughout the building, whereas furnaces burn fuel (such as natural gas, oil, or propane) to produce heat. On the other hand, heat pumps use a refrigeration cycle to move heat from the ground or external air into a building.

Ventilation is another critical aspect of HVAC systems. It focuses on the exchange of indoor and outdoor air to maintain fresh air circulation within a building. Ventilation helps remove pollutants, odors, and excess moisture from indoor spaces, ensuring better indoor air quality. Proper ventilation also plays a vital role in controlling humidity levels and preventing the buildup of harmful gasses, such as carbon monoxide. Ventilation systems commonly include air ducts, fans, and air vents to facilitate the movement of air.

Figure 1.2 Cooling Tower

Air conditioning is a key component of HVAC systems, particularly in regions with hot and humid climates. It involves the process of cooling the indoor air to a comfortable temperature and removing excess humidity. Air conditioning systems typically use refrigeration cycles to extract heat from the indoor air and transfer it outdoors. These systems consist of compressors, condensers, evaporators, and refrigerant lines to achieve the cooling effect. Air conditioning not only enhances comfort but also helps maintain stable indoor conditions, which can have a positive impact on equipment performance and the longevity of building materials.

HVAC systems can include elements like air filtration, humidity control, and energy management systems in addition to heating, ventilation, and air conditioning. By removing dust, allergens, and other airborne particles from the indoor environment, air filtration serves to improve air quality and lower the likelihood of respiratory problems. Controlling humidity is crucial for keeping the air at the right relative humidity and avoiding excessive dryness or humidity, which can be uncomfortable and unhealthy. By maximizing temperature settings and scheduling, energy management systems, such as programmable thermostats and smart controls, provide effective operation and energy savings.

Figure 1.3 Portable Ac

Understanding HVAC systems involves grasping the interaction between heating, ventilation, and air conditioning components to achieve a balanced and efficient indoor environment. These systems are designed based on various factors, including building size, insulation levels, climate conditions, and occupant requirements. By effectively controlling temperature, air quality, and humidity, HVAC systems create comfortable and healthy indoor spaces, promoting productivity, well-being, and overall quality of life.

Importance of HVAC Systems in Residential and Commercial Settings
HVAC systems are essential in both residential and business settings, offering many advantages that improve inhabitants' comfort, health, and general well-being. Regardless of the weather outside, these systems are necessary for establishing and sustaining ideal indoor environments. The significance of HVAC systems in both home and commercial settings will be discussed.

Comfort: One of the primary reasons for the significance of HVAC systems is the comfort they provide. In residential settings, HVAC systems ensure that homeowners and their families can enjoy a pleasant and comfortable living environment throughout the year. Whether it's heating during winter or cooling during summer, these systems help regulate indoor temperatures to desired levels, allowing individuals to relax, sleep, and go about their daily activities without discomfort.

Figure 1.4 Chillers Ac

In commercial settings, HVAC systems play a crucial role in creating a comfortable environment for employees, customers, and clients. Comfortable indoor temperatures contribute to improved productivity and overall satisfaction. Maintaining an optimal temperature range helps individuals focus better, reduces fatigue, and promotes a sense of well-being, ultimately enhancing work efficiency and customer experience.

Indoor air quality has a direct impact on health, therefore HVAC systems are necessary for ensuring optimum indoor air quality. In residential settings, HVAC systems assist remove pollutants, allergens, and toxins from the interior air, lowering the risk of respiratory disorders, allergies, and other health issues. It guarantees a steady flow of fresh outdoor air and the efficient expulsion of stale or contaminated air.

In commercial settings, HVAC systems contribute to the health and well-being of employees and customers by controlling indoor air quality. Efficient filtration systems in HVAC units can remove airborne particles, such as dust, pollen, and bacteria, leading to healthier indoor environments. Good air quality helps reduce the spread of airborne diseases, enhances respiratory comfort, and creates a more pleasant and productive atmosphere.

Energy Efficiency: HVAC systems have a significant impact on energy consumption in both residential and commercial buildings. Efficient HVAC systems utilize energy-saving technologies, such as high-efficiency equipment, smart controls, and zoning systems, to optimize energy usage and reduce utility costs.

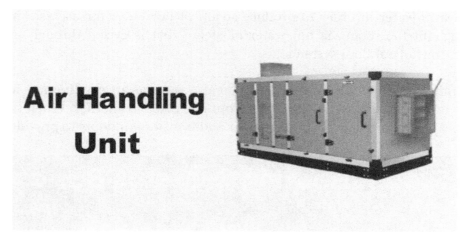

Figure 1.5 Air Handling Unit

In residential settings, energy-efficient HVAC systems can result in substantial energy savings over time. By properly sizing and maintaining the equipment, homeowners can enjoy reduced energy bills while minimizing their environmental footprint. Moreover, energy-efficient HVAC systems often qualify for government incentives and rebates, making them even more appealing to homeowners.

Equipment Longevity and Maintenance: HVAC systems require regular maintenance to ensure optimal performance and longevity. Properly maintained systems have a longer lifespan, reducing the need for premature replacements and associated costs. Residential and commercial buildings with well-maintained HVAC systems are less likely to experience unexpected breakdowns or system failures, ensuring uninterrupted comfort for occupants.

Regular maintenance of HVAC systems also includes tasks such as filter replacement, coil cleaning, and inspection of components. These maintenance activities contribute to improved system efficiency, better indoor air quality, and early detection of potential issues, preventing major breakdowns and costly repairs.

Basic Components of an HVAC System
An HVAC system comprises several essential components that work together to provide heating, ventilation, and air conditioning functions. Each component serves a specific purpose in creating a

comfortable and controlled indoor environment. Let's explore the basic components of an HVAC system:

Heating Components

Heating components in an HVAC system are responsible for raising the indoor temperature during cold weather conditions. The most common heating components include:

The most popular heating method in both residential and commercial structures is the furnace. To generate heat, they burn fuel like natural gas, oil, or propane. Air ducts and fans are then used to spread the heat throughout the entire structure.

Boilers: Boilers warm water in order to produce steam or hot water for use as a heater. Warmth is distributed throughout the room via hot water or steam that is cycled through pipes to radiators, baseboard heaters, or radiant floor systems.

Heat Pumps: Multipurpose heating systems that can also serve as air conditioners are known as heat pumps. They use refrigerant cycles to move heat from one place to another. When they are in heating mode, they pull heat from the ground or external air and transfer it indoors to provide warmth.

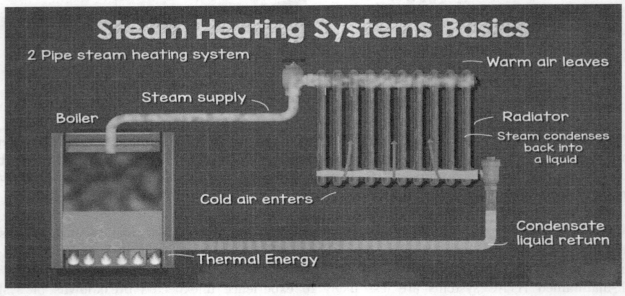

Figure 1.6 Steam Heating System

Ventilation Components

Ventilation components in an HVAC system ensure the circulation of fresh air, remove stale air, and maintain a healthy indoor environment. Key ventilation components include:

The network of channels known as air ducts is responsible for distributing conditioned air throughout the structure. They deliver heated or cooled air to various rooms and return conditioned air to the HVAC system. Air leakage is reduced and effective airflow is ensured by properly constructed and sealed ductwork.

Fans: Fans are responsible for moving air through the ventilation system. They can be found in various locations, such as within the HVAC unit, air handlers, and exhaust systems. Fans help in distributing conditioned air, providing adequate airflow, and removing stale air.

Air Vents/Registers: Air vents or registers are openings in walls, floors, or ceilings where conditioned air is delivered into a room. They can be adjusted to control the airflow and temperature within individual spaces. Air vents also play a role in maintaining balanced air pressure throughout the building.

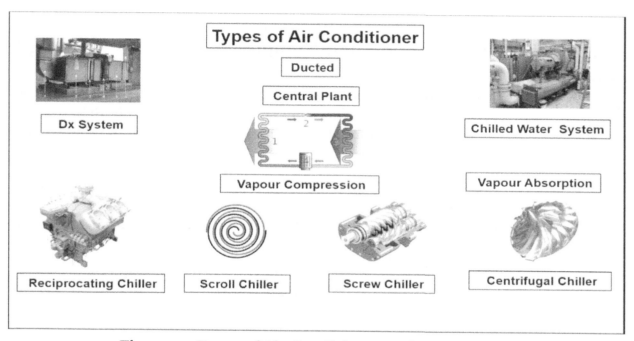

Figure 1.7 Types of Air Conditioner and Components

Air Conditioning Components

Air conditioning components are responsible for cooling the indoor air and removing excess humidity. These components are commonly used in regions with warm climates. The key air conditioning components include:

Compressors: Compressors are the heart of air conditioning systems. They compress refrigerant gasses, increasing their temperature and pressure. This process allows the refrigerant to release heat outside and prepare it for the cooling cycle.

Condensers: Condensers assist in transferring heat from indoor air to the outdoors. They help the refrigerant condense into liquid form by facilitating the heat transmission from the refrigerant to the ambient air.

Evaporators: Evaporators absorb heat from the indoor air, facilitating the cooling process. They allow the refrigerant to evaporate, absorbing heat energy and lowering the temperature of the surrounding air.

Refrigerant Lines: Refrigerant lines consist of pipes or tubing that carry the refrigerant between the various components of the air conditioning system. These lines ensure the proper flow and circulation of the refrigerant during the cooling process.

Understanding these basic components of an HVAC system provides a foundation for comprehending how heating, ventilation, and air conditioning work together to create a comfortable indoor environment. Each component plays a crucial role in regulating temperature, controlling air quality, and maintaining optimal humidity levels. By combining these components effectively

Types of HVAC Systems and Their Components

Split Systems
Split systems are a popular type of HVAC system commonly used in both residential and commercial settings. They consist of two main components: an indoor unit and an outdoor unit. Split systems offer several advantages, including flexibility in installation, efficient operation, and the ability to provide heating and cooling capabilities.

The indoor unit of a split system contains the components responsible for air distribution and conditioning within the building. It typically consists of an air handler or an evaporator coil, a fan, and controls. The outdoor unit houses the compressor, condenser coil, and other components required for heat transfer and heat exchange with the outdoor environment.

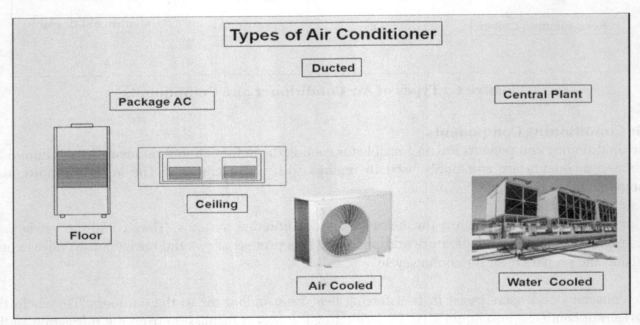

Figure 1.8 Types of Air Conditioner

Components of a Split System

Indoor Unit:

Air Handler/Evaporator Coil: The air handler or evaporator coil is responsible for cooling the indoor air. It contains refrigerant-filled coils that absorb heat from the indoor air, cooling it in the process.

Figure 1.9 Fan Coil unit

- Fan: The fan inside the indoor unit circulates the conditioned air throughout the building. It helps in maintaining a consistent airflow and distributing cool or warm air to different rooms.
- Controls: The controls, such as thermostats or programmable controllers, are located on the indoor unit and allow users to set and regulate the desired temperature and control other operational features of the split system.

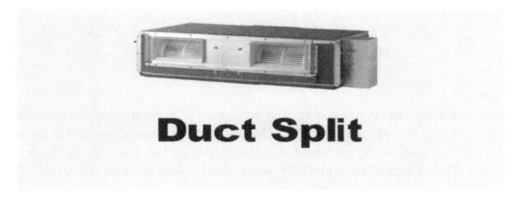

Figure 1.10 Duct Split

Outdoor Unit:

- Compressor: An essential part of the outside unit is the compressor. In order to facilitate effective heat exchange, it pressurizes the refrigerant, raising its temperature and pressure.
- Condenser Coil: The condenser coil is in charge of dissipating the heat that has been absorbed from the indoor air outside. It makes it easier for heat to be transferred from the refrigerant to the ambient air, resulting in the condensing of the refrigerant into a liquid.
- Expansion Valve: The expansion valve is located in the outdoor unit and helps regulate the flow of refrigerant between the indoor and outdoor units. It controls the refrigerant's pressure and temperature, allowing for efficient cooling or heating operation.

- Refrigerant Lines: Refrigerant lines connect the indoor and outdoor units, carrying the refrigerant between them. These lines ensure the proper flow and circulation of the refrigerant during the cooling or heating process.

Split systems are known for their quiet operation, as the noisy components, such as the compressor, are located in the outdoor unit. This design minimizes indoor noise levels and provides a more peaceful environment.

Split systems offer flexibility in terms of capacity, allowing for zoning and temperature control in different areas of the building. By installing multiple indoor units connected to a single outdoor unit, occupants can adjust the temperature independently in various zones, optimizing energy usage and comfort.

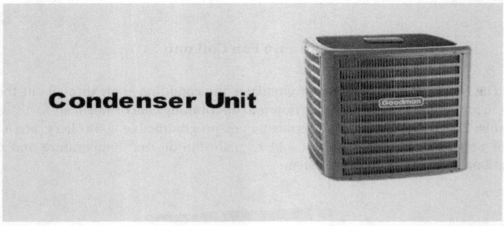

Figure 1.11 Outdoor Condenser Unit

Packaged Systems
Packaged systems are a type of HVAC system that combines all the necessary heating, ventilation, and air conditioning components into a single unit. Unlike split systems where the components are split between indoor and outdoor units, packaged systems house all the components together in a single, compact enclosure. This design offers simplicity in installation and efficient operation.

Components of a Packaged System

Heating Components:

- Gas or Electric Heating Elements: Packaged systems can incorporate gas or electric heating elements to provide warmth during colder months. Gas-powered systems utilize burners and heat exchangers to generate warm air, while electric heating elements use electrical resistance to produce heat.
- Heat Exchanger: The heat exchanger transfers heat from the combustion process or electrical resistance to the air that will be circulated throughout the building. It ensures efficient heating and prevents the mixing of combustion byproducts with the indoor air.

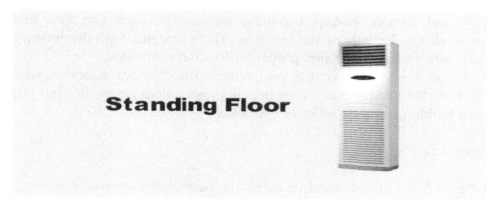

Figure 1.12 Standing Cooling Components System

Cooling Components:

- Compressor: The compressor is a crucial component of the cooling system in a packaged unit. It compresses the refrigerant, raising its temperature and pressure for effective heat transfer.
- Condenser Coil: The condenser coil aids in transferring heat from the indoor environment to the outside atmosphere. It makes it easier for heat to be transferred from the refrigerant to the ambient air, resulting in the liquidization of the refrigerant.
- Expansion Valve: The expansion valve regulates the flow of refrigerant, controlling its pressure and temperature. It is responsible for metering the refrigerant into the evaporator coil.
- Evaporator Coil: The evaporator coil cools the inside air by absorbing heat from it. It enables the refrigerant to evaporate, capturing heat energy and bringing down the ambient air's temperature.

Figure 1.13 Water Cooler

Ventilation Components:

11

- Air Supply and Return: Packaged systems include ductwork and fans that circulate and distribute fresh air throughout the building. These systems typically incorporate supply air vents and return air vents to ensure proper airflow and ventilation.
- Air Filters: Air filters are essential components that remove airborne particles, dust, and pollutants from the incoming air. They help improve indoor air quality and protect the system from debris buildup, ensuring efficient operation.

Controls and Thermostats:

- Control Panel: The control panel contains the necessary switches, sensors, and controls to operate and regulate the packaged system. It allows users to adjust settings, monitor temperatures, and control the system's operation.
- Thermostats: Thermostats serve as the user interface for controlling the temperature and settings of the packaged system. They enable occupants to set their desired comfort levels and can be programmed for energy-saving operation.

Figure 1.14 Cooler Concealed

Packaged systems are commonly used in small to medium-sized buildings, such as single-family homes, small offices, retail stores, and light commercial spaces. They offer a convenient and efficient solution by integrating all HVAC components into a single unit. The compact design, ease of installation, and flexibility make packaged systems a popular choice in situations where space is limited or when a centralized HVAC system is desired.

Hybrid Systems
Hybrid systems are innovative HVAC systems that combine multiple technologies to optimize energy efficiency and provide effective heating and cooling. These systems integrate the benefits of different heating and cooling sources, such as traditional furnaces, heat pumps, and renewable energy systems. The goal of hybrid systems is to maximize energy savings while maintaining optimal comfort levels. They are designed to adapt to changing climate conditions and energy costs by utilizing a combination of heating and cooling sources. The system intelligently switches between different heating and cooling modes based on factors such as outdoor temperature, energy prices, and system efficiency. By

selecting the most efficient energy source for each situation, hybrid systems can significantly reduce energy consumption and operational costs.

Components of Hybrid Systems

Heat Pump: The heat pump is a vital part of hybrid systems. Heat pumps are very effective appliances that may be used for both cooling and heating. When in cooling mode, they remove heat from the air inside and send it outside, effectively cooling the inside. When in heating mode, they take heat from the ground or external air and transmit it indoors, warming the space. Heat pumps are a great option for hybrid systems since they work more efficiently than conventional heating systems.

Furnace: Hybrid systems often incorporate a traditional furnace as a supplemental heating source. Furnaces are typically powered by natural gas, oil, or propane and provide reliable and consistent heat output. When outdoor temperatures drop to a point where the heat pump's efficiency decreases, the hybrid system activates the furnace to ensure efficient and effective heating.

Renewable Energy Sources: Hybrid systems can incorporate renewable energy sources like solar panels or geothermal systems to further improve energy efficiency and sustainability. These sources add to the system's heating and cooling requirements by utilizing renewable energy from the sun or the earth. Hybrid systems lessen dependency on conventional energy sources and help create a greener world by using clean and renewable energy.

Control System: Hybrid systems rely on advanced control systems to monitor outdoor temperatures, energy prices, and system efficiency. These control systems intelligently determine the most efficient heating or cooling source to use at any given time. They also allow users to set desired comfort levels, schedule operation, and access energy consumption data for better management of the system.

Hybrid systems are a promising solution for achieving energy-efficient and sustainable HVAC operations. By combining the strengths of different heating and cooling sources, these systems provide optimal comfort, significant energy savings, and environmental benefits.

Geothermal Systems
Ground-source heat pump systems, commonly referred to as geothermal systems, are cutting-edge and environmentally friendly HVAC systems that use the heat from the Earth to provide heating, cooling, and hot water. These systems effectively transmit heat energy by taking advantage of the constant subsurface temperatures, resulting in exceptional energy savings and sustainability. The ground loop, heat pump, and distribution system make up their three primary parts.

The geothermal system's beating heart is the ground loop. Depending on the available area, it consists of a number of pipes buried underground, either horizontally or vertically. These heat-transfer fluid-filled high-density polyethylene pipes are commonly filled with a solution of water and antifreeze. When in heating mode, the ground loop absorbs heat from the ground; when in cooling mode, it rejects heat to the ground. Ground loops can be of two typical types:

- Horizontal Loop: This configuration is used when sufficient land area is available. The pipes are installed in trenches, typically 4-6 feet deep, and are horizontally spaced apart.
- Vertical Loop: Vertical loops are employed when space is limited. In this setup, pipes are inserted vertically into boreholes that can range from 100 to 400 feet deep.

Another crucial element of geothermal systems is the heat pump. The building is heated or cooled using the heat energy from the ground loop. The heat pump draws heat from the ground loop during the heating mode and amplifies it to a higher temperature that is adequate for warming the inside space. The process is reversed in the cooling mode, with the heat pump removing heat from the building and transferring it to the ground loop to efficiently chill the inside.

The heat pump employs a refrigeration cycle similar to that of an air conditioner or a refrigerator. It consists of a compressor, evaporator coil, condenser coil, and expansion valve. The heat pump's operation is highly efficient, as it relies on the consistent ground temperatures, which remain relatively constant compared to outdoor air temperatures.

Distribution System:
The distribution system in a geothermal system is responsible for delivering the heated or cooled air to different areas of the building. It typically consists of air ducts or radiant flooring systems. Air ducts distribute conditioned air throughout the building, while radiant flooring systems use hot water or electric coils embedded in the floor to provide warmth.

Principles of Heat Transfer in HVAC Systems

Heat transfer is a fundamental concept in HVAC systems that plays a crucial role in the heating, cooling, and ventilation processes. Understanding the principles of heat transfer is essential for designing, operating, and optimizing HVAC systems to achieve efficient and comfortable indoor environments. By optimizing heat transfer processes, HVAC systems can minimize energy consumption, reduce operational costs, and create comfortable and sustainable indoor environments.

Conduction
Conduction is the process of heat transfer through direct contact between materials or substances. In HVAC systems, conduction occurs when heat flows from a region of higher temperature to a region of lower temperature within a solid object or between two objects in contact. The rate of heat conduction depends on the thermal conductivity of the materials involved. Materials with high thermal conductivity, such as metals, allow heat to transfer more easily compared to materials with low thermal conductivity, like insulating materials. Proper insulation is essential to minimize heat loss or gain through conduction, ensuring energy efficiency in HVAC systems.

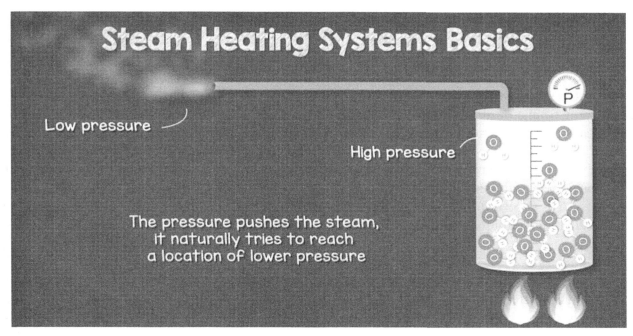

Figure 1.15 Heat transferred System

Convection

Heat is transferred via convection when fluids, like air or water, are moving. Convection is a key component of the heating and cooling processes in HVAC systems. Natural convection and forced convection are the two types of convection.

Natural convection: This occurs when heat is transferred through the buoyancy of fluid due to density differences caused by temperature variations. For example, in a heating system, warm air rises while cooler air descends, creating a natural convection loop. In cooling systems, the opposite occurs. Proper design considerations, such as the placement of heating or cooling sources and air circulation patterns, can enhance natural convection and improve overall system efficiency.

Forced convection: This involves the use of mechanical devices, such as fans or blowers, to facilitate the movement of fluid and enhance heat transfer. Forced convection increases the rate of heat exchange by promoting better fluid circulation and maximizing the contact between the fluid and the heated or cooled surfaces. HVAC systems often utilize forced convection to distribute conditioned air throughout a space, ensuring efficient heating, cooling, and ventilation.

Radiation

Heat can be transferred through electromagnetic waves without a medium thanks to radiation. Radiation can take place in a vacuum, in contrast to conduction and convection. When heat is emitted or absorbed by surfaces without direct touch, radiation happens in HVAC systems. An illustration of natural radiation is the sun's transmission of heat to Earth. Thermal radiation can affect indoor comfort and energy efficiency in HVAC applications. For instance, solar radiation can cause a building to heat up, whereas items can cool down by radiating heat into cooler surroundings. Radiant heat transmission in HVAC systems can be controlled through the wise selection of surface materials with high or low emissivity and the use of reflective surfaces.

Latent Heat Transfer

Latent heat transfer refers to the heat that is transferred when a substance undergoes a phase shift, such as going from a solid to a liquid or from a liquid to a gas. Latent heat transmission is crucial to the humidification and dehumidification processes in HVAC systems. Latent heat transfer happens when moisture is added to or withdrawn from the air, impacting the room's overall thermal comfort. For instance, when moisture condenses on an air conditioner's evaporator coil during the cooling process, latent heat is released. On the other hand, as the air is humidified, latent heat is absorbed as water evaporates. To successfully manage latent heat transmission, appropriate humidification and dehumidification techniques are required.

Heat Exchangers

Heat exchangers are crucial components in HVAC systems that facilitate the transfer of heat energy between two fluid streams without mixing them. They play a vital role in various applications, such as in heating systems, cooling systems, and ventilation systems. Heat exchangers maximize heat transfer efficiency by increasing the surface area available for heat exchange and ensuring proper flow rates of the fluids involved. There are different types of heat exchangers, including air-to-air, water-to-air, and water-to-water heat exchangers, each suited for specific HVAC applications. The design and selection of heat exchangers depend on factors such as heat load requirements, fluid characteristics, and system efficiency goals.

Understanding the principles of conduction, convection, radiation, latent heat transfer, and heat exchangers is essential for HVAC engineers and technicians to design, operate, and optimize HVAC systems effectively. By considering these principles, HVAC systems can be designed to provide efficient heating, cooling, and ventilation while maintaining desired comfort levels. Additionally, optimizing heat transfer processes in HVAC systems leads to reduced energy consumption, lower operational costs, and the creation of comfortable and sustainable indoor environments.

HVAC Load Calculation and Equipment Sizing

Importance of Load Calculation in HVAC System Design
Load calculation is a critical process in HVAC system design as it determines the heating and cooling requirements of a space. Accurate load calculations are essential for selecting appropriately sized equipment, optimizing energy efficiency, and ensuring optimal comfort levels. There's a plethora of reasons for the importance of load calculation:

Right-Sized Equipment: Load calculation helps determine the appropriate capacity and size of HVAC equipment needed to meet the heating and cooling demands of a space. Undersized equipment may struggle to maintain comfortable temperatures, leading to inadequate cooling or heating. On the other hand, oversized equipment can result in frequent on/off cycles, inefficient operation, higher energy consumption, and reduced equipment lifespan. Accurate load calculation ensures that HVAC equipment is correctly sized, maximizing energy efficiency, and ensuring optimal system performance.

Energy Efficiency: By accurately assessing the heating and cooling load, load calculation helps optimize energy efficiency. Oversized equipment not only consumes more energy but may also cycle on and off frequently, leading to energy waste. Conversely, undersized equipment may run continuously, straining the system and increasing energy consumption. Properly sized equipment based on load calculation ensures that energy is utilized efficiently, reducing energy waste and operating costs.

Enhanced Comfort: To evaluate the heating and cooling needs of a space, load calculations take into account variables including climate, building orientation, insulation levels, occupancy, and internal heat gain. HVAC systems can provide the necessary heating and cooling capacity to sustain cozy inside temperatures all year round by precisely estimating the load. A comfortable and pleasing indoor atmosphere is ensured by proper load calculation, which helps prevent temperature imbalances, drafts, and other comfort difficulties.

Optimal Air Distribution and Ventilation: Load calculation considers the airflow requirements for proper air distribution and ventilation. It helps determine the appropriate size and location of supply and return air registers, ductwork design, and ventilation rates based on the specific load conditions. Proper air distribution and ventilation contribute to improved indoor air quality, moisture control, and occupant comfort.

Factors affecting Load Calculation
Building Orientation and Design: The orientation and design of a building influence the amount of solar heat gain, exposure to prevailing winds, and heat transfer through walls, windows, and roofs. Load calculation takes into account these factors to determine the heating and cooling load requirements accurately.

Insulation and Building Envelope: The quality and effectiveness of insulation, along with the thermal properties of the building envelope, impact heat gain and loss. Proper insulation reduces heat transfer through walls, ceilings, floors, and windows, resulting in lower heating and cooling loads.

Climate and Outdoor Conditions: Climate plays a crucial role in load calculation. The local climate, including temperature extremes, humidity levels, and seasonal variations, affects the heating and cooling load requirements. Outdoor conditions such as solar radiation, wind speed, and outdoor air temperature are also considered in load calculations.

Internal Heat Gain: Load calculation accounts for internal heat sources within a space, such as lighting, appliances, electronics, and human occupancy. These factors contribute to the overall heat load and help determine the appropriate cooling capacity required.

Infiltration and Ventilation: Air leakage through cracks, gaps, and poorly sealed openings in the building envelope affects load calculation. Load calculations consider the infiltration rate and ventilation requirements to ensure proper ventilation and account for any additional heating or cooling load associated with air leakage.

Accurate load calculation is essential for properly sizing HVAC equipment, optimizing energy efficiency, and ensuring optimal comfort levels in a space. By considering factors such as building orientation, insulation, climate, internal heat gain, and ventilation, load calculation provides the foundation for efficient HVAC system design and operation. It helps in selecting the right equipment, minimizing energy waste, reducing operating costs, and creating a comfortable indoor environment.

Heat Gain and Heat Loss Calculations
Heat gain and heat loss calculations are essential components of load calculation in HVAC system design. They involve determining the amount of heat that enters or leaves a space, considering various factors such as climate, building materials, insulation, occupancy, and equipment. These calculations provide valuable insights into the heating and cooling requirements of a space, enabling the selection of appropriately sized HVAC equipment. Here's an overview of heat gain and heat loss calculations:

Heat Gain: The amount of heat that enters a place, typically from external sources, is referred to as heat gain. Solar radiation, ambient temperature, air infiltration, interior heat sources (lighting, appliances, inhabitants), and conductive/convective heat transfer via the building envelope are some of the elements that are considered. Calculating the cooling load needed using heat gain ensures that the HVAC system can remove the heat produced in the room effectively.

Heat Loss: Heat loss refers to the amount of heat that leaves a space, primarily due to temperature differences between the inside and outside environments. It considers factors such as outdoor temperature, building insulation, air leakage, and conductive/convective heat transfer through the building envelope. Heat loss calculations help determine the heating load requirements, ensuring that the HVAC system can provide sufficient heat to maintain comfortable indoor temperatures.

Heat gain and heat loss calculations are typically performed using computer software programs or manual calculation methods. These calculations take into account specific data related to the building, including dimensions, construction materials, insulation levels, window areas, and climate conditions. By accurately assessing heat gain and heat loss, HVAC professionals can design systems that are properly sized to meet the heating and cooling demands of the space, resulting in efficient and effective operation.

Determining the appropriate HVAC Equipment size based on Load Calculation Results
Once heat gain and heat loss calculations are completed, the next step is to determine the appropriate HVAC equipment size based on the load calculation results. Proper equipment sizing is crucial for achieving optimal system performance, energy efficiency, and comfort. Here's how load calculation results guide equipment sizing:

Cooling Equipment Sizing: For cooling equipment, load calculation results provide the cooling load requirements in terms of BTUs (British Thermal Units) or tons. The cooling capacity of air conditioners or heat pumps is typically expressed in tons, with each ton representing a specific cooling capacity. Load calculation results help identify the appropriate tonnage required to meet the cooling load, considering factors such as solar heat gain, internal heat sources, and thermal characteristics of the building.

Heating Equipment Sizing: For heating equipment, load calculation results provide the heating load requirements in terms of BTUs or kilowatts. The heating capacity of furnaces, boilers, or heat pumps is typically expressed in BTUs or kilowatts. Load calculation results guide the selection of the appropriate heating capacity, considering factors such as heat loss, outdoor temperature, insulation, and thermal characteristics of the building.

It is important to note that selecting HVAC equipment solely based on square footage or rule-of-thumb estimations may result in undersized or oversized systems, leading to inefficient operation and compromised comfort. Load calculation results provide a more accurate understanding of the heating and cooling requirements, ensuring that the HVAC equipment is correctly sized to match the load, maximizing energy efficiency and system performance.

Energy Efficiency and Sustainability in HVAC Systems

Importance of Energy Efficiency in HVAC Systems
Due to its considerable effects on the economy and the environment, energy efficiency in HVAC systems is of the utmost importance. In residential, commercial, and industrial buildings, HVAC systems—which include heating, ventilation, and air conditioning—consume a significant amount of energy. Therefore, increasing HVAC system energy efficiency is essential for a number of reasons.

Reduced Energy Consumption: Energy-efficient HVAC systems consume less energy while providing the same level of heating, cooling, and ventilation. By implementing energy-efficient technologies and practices, such as high-efficiency equipment, advanced controls, and optimized system designs, energy consumption can be significantly reduced. This not only lowers energy bills for building owners and occupants but also reduces the demand for energy generation, resulting in decreased greenhouse gas emissions and environmental impact.

Lower Operating Costs: Energy-efficient HVAC systems help to lower operating costs for building owners and occupants. By reducing energy consumption, these systems can result in substantial savings over the system's lifespan. The investment in energy-efficient technologies and practices can often be recouped through energy cost savings in a relatively short period. Furthermore, energy-efficient systems often require less maintenance and repair, further contributing to cost savings.

Environmental Benefits: HVAC systems account for a significant portion of global energy consumption and greenhouse gas emissions. By improving energy efficiency in these systems, we can mitigate the environmental impact associated with energy production and consumption. Energy-efficient HVAC systems help to reduce carbon dioxide (CO_2) emissions, decrease reliance on fossil fuels, and contribute to overall sustainability efforts.

Enhanced Comfort and Indoor Air Quality: Energy-efficient HVAC systems not only save energy but also improve comfort and indoor air quality. These systems can deliver consistent and precise temperature control, balanced airflow, and effective humidity control. Enhanced comfort and indoor air quality contribute to a healthier and more productive indoor environment for occupants.

Regulatory Compliance and Incentives: Governments and regulatory bodies around the world are increasingly implementing energy efficiency standards and regulations. Compliance with these standards ensures that HVAC systems meet minimum energy performance requirements. In addition, many jurisdictions offer incentives, rebates, or tax credits to encourage the adoption of energy-efficient technologies, making it financially beneficial for building owners to invest in energy-efficient HVAC systems.

Future-Proofing Buildings: Energy efficiency is becoming a critical factor in building design, construction, and operation. As energy costs continue to rise, environmental concerns become more pressing, and sustainability becomes a priority, energy-efficient HVAC systems will play a crucial role in future-proofing buildings. By investing in energy efficiency today, building owners can ensure that their properties remain competitive, resilient, and environmentally responsible in the face of evolving energy regulations and market demands.

Energy-efficient HVAC Technologies and Strategies

Energy efficiency is a key consideration in designing, operating, and maintaining HVAC systems. By incorporating energy-efficient technologies and implementing effective strategies, significant energy savings can be achieved while ensuring optimal comfort and performance. Here are some energy-efficient HVAC technologies and strategies that contribute to improved efficiency and sustainability:

High-Efficiency Equipment: One of the most important ways to increase energy efficiency is by using high-efficiency HVAC equipment. Energy consumption can be greatly decreased by using energy-efficient heating systems, such as condensing boilers or heat pumps with high Seasonal Energy Efficiency Ratio (SEER) and Annual Fuel Utilization Efficiency (AFUE) ratings. Similar to this, high-efficiency HVAC systems with sophisticated controls and variable-speed motors can adjust temperature and airflow precisely while using the least amount of energy.

Building Automation Systems (BAS): Implementing advanced building automation systems enables centralized control and monitoring of HVAC systems. BAS utilize sophisticated algorithms to optimize system performance based on real-time data, occupancy schedules, and weather conditions. By integrating various components such as thermostats, sensors, and actuators, BAS can regulate HVAC operation, identify energy-saving opportunities, and enable proactive maintenance.

Demand-Controlled Ventilation (DCV): DCV systems adjust ventilation rates based on actual occupancy levels, optimizing airflow while reducing unnecessary energy consumption. These systems use occupancy sensors or carbon dioxide (CO_2) sensors to modulate the ventilation rates accordingly. By providing fresh air in response to actual occupancy, DCV ensures indoor air quality while minimizing energy waste associated with excessive ventilation.

Variable Air Volume (VAV) Systems: VAV systems adjust the airflow based on the specific cooling or heating demands of different zones within a building. By utilizing variable-speed fans and modulating dampers, VAV systems deliver the required airflow precisely, avoiding over-conditioning and reducing energy usage. Zoning strategies within VAV systems further enhance energy efficiency by allowing individual control of temperature in different areas, optimizing comfort while minimizing energy waste.

Ventilation systems that recover heat or energy from exhaust air and transfer it to incoming fresh air are known as heat recovery ventilation (HRV) and energy recovery ventilation (ERV). While ERV systems recover both heat and moisture, HRV systems only recover heat. HRV and ERV systems reduce the stress on heating and cooling equipment by preheating or precooling the fresh air with energy from the exhaust air, resulting in energy savings.

Proper System Commissioning and Maintenance: Regular system commissioning and maintenance play a crucial role in ensuring energy efficiency. Properly calibrated controls, clean filters, balanced airflow, and well-maintained equipment contribute to optimal system performance and energy efficiency. Regular inspections, tune-ups, and preventive maintenance help identify and address potential issues, ensuring that HVAC systems operate at peak efficiency.

Building Envelope Improvements: Upgrading insulation, sealing air leaks, and improving windows and doors contribute to reduced heat gain and heat loss, reducing the workload on HVAC systems. By enhancing the building envelope's thermal performance, energy consumption can be significantly minimized, improving overall energy efficiency.

Occupant Engagement and Education: Encouraging occupants to adopt energy-conscious behaviors, such as setting appropriate temperatures, utilizing natural ventilation when possible, and turning off equipment when not in use, can have a significant impact on energy efficiency. Educating occupants about the importance of energy conservation and providing energy-saving tips empowers them to actively contribute to reducing energy consumption.

By incorporating these energy-efficient HVAC technologies and strategies, building owners and operators can achieve substantial energy savings, lower operating costs, and contribute to sustainability efforts. Combining efficient equipment, advanced controls, optimal system design, and proactive maintenance leads to a more sustainable built environment while providing a comfortable and healthy indoor space for occupants.

Environmental Considerations and Sustainability in HVAC Systems
Designing and running HVAC systems must take sustainability and the environment into account. Sustainability strategies and technology must be used because HVAC systems contribute significantly to energy use and greenhouse gas emissions. The following are some essential sustainability and environmental considerations for HVAC systems:

Reduced Carbon Footprint: The energy use of HVAC systems increases carbon dioxide (CO_2) emissions. The carbon footprint of HVAC systems can be greatly decreased by emphasizing energy efficiency and employing renewable energy sources. This entails putting in place energy-efficient machinery, improving system layouts, and incorporating renewable energy sources like solar energy or geothermal heat pumps.

The choice of refrigerants matters because they can have a big influence on the environment when used in HVAC systems. The ozone layer is known to be destroyed by conventional refrigerants like chlorofluorocarbons (CFCs) and hydrochlorofluorocarbons (HCFCs), which also have a significant global warming potential (GWP). By using environmentally friendly refrigerants, such as hydrofluorocarbons (HFCs) with low GWP or natural refrigerants like hydrocarbons or carbon dioxide

(CO2), one can promote sustainability and lessen environmental impact. These refrigerants have lower or zero ozone depletion potential (ODP) and global warming potential (GWP).

HVAC systems can be given a life cycle assessment (LCA) to determine their environmental impact across their entire life cycle, from production and installation to usage and disposal. Making informed decisions that prioritize sustainability requires taking into account aspects including energy use, material sourcing, manufacturing techniques, and end-of-life disposal. LCA identifies areas that can be improved, such as choosing materials with less embodied energy or creating systems that are simple to disassemble and recycle.

Water Conservation: While HVAC systems primarily focus on heating, ventilation, and air conditioning, water conservation should also be considered. Water-cooled HVAC equipment and humidification systems can consume significant amounts of water. Implementing water-saving strategies, such as using closed-loop cooling systems or reclaiming and reusing condensate water, reduces water consumption and promotes sustainability.

Indoor Air Quality (IAQ): Achieving good indoor air quality is an essential aspect of sustainable HVAC systems. Proper ventilation, filtration, and humidity control are necessary to maintain a healthy and comfortable indoor environment. High-efficiency filters can remove particulate matter, allergens, and pollutants, improving IAQ. Additionally, utilizing natural ventilation strategies, such as operable windows or natural airflow design, promotes sustainability by reducing the reliance on mechanical ventilation.

Smart Controls and Building Integration: Incorporating smart controls and integrating HVAC systems with building management systems (BMS) enables more efficient operation. By leveraging real-time data, occupancy sensors, and weather forecasts, HVAC systems can adapt to changing conditions and optimize energy consumption. Smart controls can automatically adjust temperature setpoints, airflow rates, and ventilation levels based on occupancy, improving comfort while minimizing energy waste.

Sustainable Materials and Construction: When installing or retrofitting HVAC systems, choosing sustainable materials and construction practices can contribute to environmental sustainability. This includes selecting materials with low embodied energy, utilizing recycled or renewable materials, and employing construction techniques that minimize waste generation and energy consumption. Sustainable HVAC system installation considers the overall environmental impact, from equipment selection to the disposal of construction debris.

Maintenance and System Optimization: Regular maintenance and system optimization are crucial for ensuring long-term sustainability. Proper maintenance practices, including filter replacement, coil cleaning, and equipment tune-ups, help maintain optimal system efficiency and performance. Additionally, periodic system optimization through commissioning and retro-commissioning identifies energy-saving opportunities, ensures proper system operation, and maximizes efficiency.

Book 2

HVAC Installation and Maintenance

Tools and Equipment for HVAC Installation

Essential HVAC Installation Tools
When it comes to HVAC installation, having the right tools is crucial for ensuring a successful and efficient job. These essential HVAC installation tools enable technicians to properly handle various tasks, from equipment assembly to system troubleshooting. Here are some of the key tools you'll need to have in your HVAC toolkit:

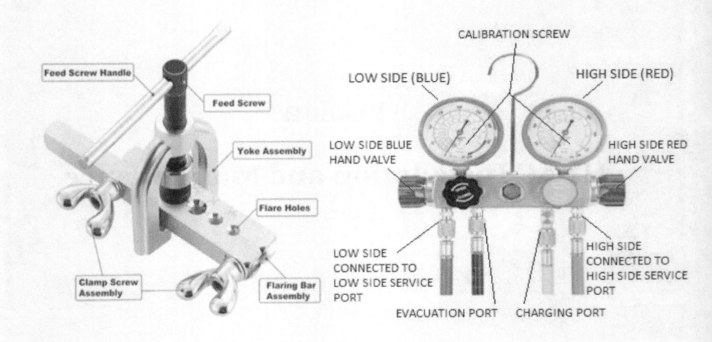

Figure 2.1 HVAC Installation Tools

Screwdrivers and Pliers: Screwdrivers in various sizes and types (flathead and Phillips) are essential for loosening or tightening screws and fasteners. Pliers, including needle-nose and adjustable pliers, come in handy for gripping and manipulating wires, small components, and fittings.

Wrenches and Spanners: Wrenches are indispensable for tightening or loosening nuts, bolts, and pipe fittings. Adjustable wrenches allow for versatility when dealing with different sizes. Additionally, pipe wrenches are specifically designed to grip and turn pipes securely.

Measuring and Testing Tools: Accurate measurements and proper testing are vital in HVAC installation. Some essential measuring and testing tools include:

- Tape Measure: Used to measure distances, duct lengths, and clearances.
- Digital Thermometer: Measures temperature differentials and helps assess system performance.

- Manometer: Measures air pressure differentials, ensuring proper airflow.
- Anemometer: Determines air velocity and flow rates within ducts.
- Combustion Analyzer: Assesses the combustion efficiency of furnaces and boilers.

Cutting and Fabrication Tools: HVAC installation often requires cutting and fabricating various materials. The essential cutting and fabrication tools include:

- Tubing Cutter: Enables clean and precise cuts on copper, aluminum, and plastic tubing.
- Pipe Cutter: Used for cutting steel, stainless steel, and cast iron pipes.
- Tin Snips: Ideal for cutting sheet metal and ductwork.
- Hole Saw Kit: Allows for creating holes of various sizes in ducts and materials.
- Flaring Tool: Essential for creating flare fittings on copper tubing.

Electrical Tools: Proper electrical work is integral to HVAC installation. Some essential electrical tools include:

- Multimeter: Used to measure voltage, current, and resistance during electrical troubleshooting.
- Wire Strippers and Cutters: Essential for stripping insulation from wires and cutting them to length.
- Wire Crimpers: Used for creating secure connections with electrical terminals.
- Voltage Tester: Ensures the presence or absence of electrical voltage for safety purposes.
- Circuit Tester: Allows for testing circuits and identifying electrical issues.

Having these essential HVAC installation tools in your arsenal will provide you with the necessary equipment to handle a wide range of tasks. Remember to invest in high-quality tools from reputable brands to ensure durability and accuracy. By having the right tools at your disposal, you can work efficiently and effectively while ensuring the proper installation of heating, ventilation, and air conditioning systems.

Specialized Equipment for HVAC Installation
In addition to the essential HVAC installation tools, there are specialized equipment and instruments designed specifically for handling the intricacies of heating, ventilation, and air conditioning systems. These specialized tools not only make the installation process more efficient but also ensure the accuracy and reliability of the final result. Let's explore some of the key specialized equipment used in HVAC installation:

Vacuum Pumps and Manifolds: Vacuum pumps are crucial for removing moisture and air from the refrigerant lines during system installation or repair. They create a vacuum within the system, allowing for proper refrigerant charging. Manifolds, on the other hand, are sets of gauges, valves, and hoses used to measure and control pressure during refrigerant evacuation and charging processes.

Recovery Machines: Recovery machines are essential for removing refrigerants from HVAC systems that need repair or decommissioning. These machines safely collect and store refrigerants to prevent their release into the environment. It is important to adhere to environmental regulations and industry best practices when handling refrigerant recovery.

Refrigerant Scales and Charging Kits: To ensure proper refrigerant charging, refrigerant scales are used to accurately measure the amount of refrigerant being added to the system. Charging kits often include hoses, gauges, and adapters necessary for connecting the refrigerant container to the system and controlling the charging process. Precise refrigerant charging is critical for achieving optimal system performance.

Pipe and Tube Benders: Pipe and tube benders are specialized tools used for shaping and bending metal pipes and tubing. In HVAC installation, these tools are particularly useful for bending copper or aluminum refrigerant lines and condensate drain lines to fit specific configurations and spatial constraints. Properly bent pipes and tubing contribute to efficient system operation and minimize refrigerant leaks.

Leak Detection Tools: Detecting refrigerant leaks is crucial for ensuring system performance, energy efficiency, and environmental compliance. Various specialized leak detection tools are available, including electronic leak detectors, UV dye kits, and bubble solutions. These tools help pinpoint leaks in refrigerant lines, fittings, coils, and other components, allowing for timely repairs and preventing further damage.

Having access to specialized HVAC installation equipment is essential for achieving high-quality results. It not only simplifies complex tasks but also enhances system performance, safety, and longevity. It's important to familiarize yourself with the manufacturer's instructions and safety guidelines when using specialized equipment to ensure proper operation and prevent accidents or damage to the HVAC system.

Investing in quality specialized equipment will not only enhance your efficiency and accuracy but also contribute to your professional reputation. By utilizing these specialized tools, you can confidently tackle the challenges of HVAC installation, provide reliable solutions to your clients, and ensure the longevity and optimal performance of heating, ventilation, and air conditioning systems.

Ductwork Design and Installation

Ductwork, a fundamental component in heating, ventilation, and air conditioning (HVAC) systems, assumes a pivotal role by transporting conditioned air to distinct sections of a building. Effective ductwork design and installation require a comprehensive grasp of its constituent elements, each of which serves a distinct purpose and collectively impacts the HVAC system's overall performance and efficiency. Let us delve into the key technical aspects of ductwork components:

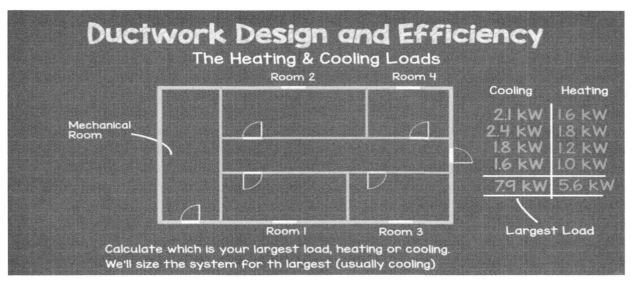

Figure 2.2 Heating and Cooling Ductwork Design

Supply and Return Ducts: Supply ducts function as conduits for delivering conditioned air from the HVAC system's air handler or furnace to various rooms or zones within the building. Conversely, return ducts retrieve air from the conditioned space and direct it back to the HVAC system for further processing. The appropriate balance and functionality of both supply and return ducts are critical for maintaining optimal air circulation and comfort.

Registers and Grilles: The discernible elements of the ductwork, encompassing the openings through which conditioned air enters or exits a room, are denoted as registers and grilles. Residents can adjust the louvers or dampers on registers to regulate the airflow's direction and intensity. Although registers and grilles share a similar function, grilles are more commonly employed in scenarios requiring higher airflows or aesthetic considerations.

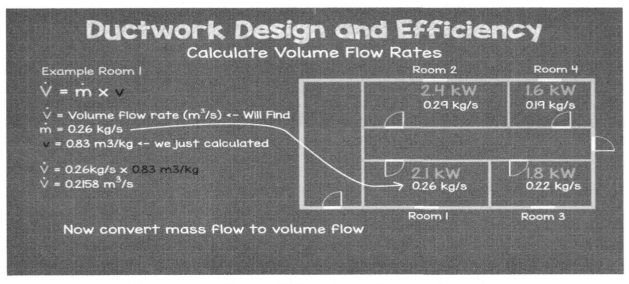

Figure 2.3 Volume of Flow Rates Ductwork Design

Plenums and Transitions: Plenums, acting as chambers or compartments in the ductwork, play a vital role in uniformly distributing air to multiple outlets. These transitional spaces mediate between the main supply or return ducts and individual branch ducts. Transitions, comprising curved or angled sections, enable seamless changes in airflow direction, such as transitioning from a rectangular main duct to a round branch duct.

Dampers and Diffusers: Dampers, in the form of movable plates or blades within the ductwork, permit airflow regulation and control. Their usage is prominent in balancing airflow distribution to different zones or rooms, ensuring optimal comfort and energy efficiency. Diffusers, on the other hand, disperse conditioned air evenly throughout occupied spaces, often integrating fins or louvers to minimize drafts and facilitate effective air distribution.

Grasping these intricacies of ductwork components forms the bedrock of efficient and balanced system design. The selection and placement of each component hinge on factors like airflow requirements, system capacity, and architectural constraints. Prudent ductwork design and installation guarantee the effective and efficient conveyance of conditioned air, maximizing comfort levels and energy conservation.

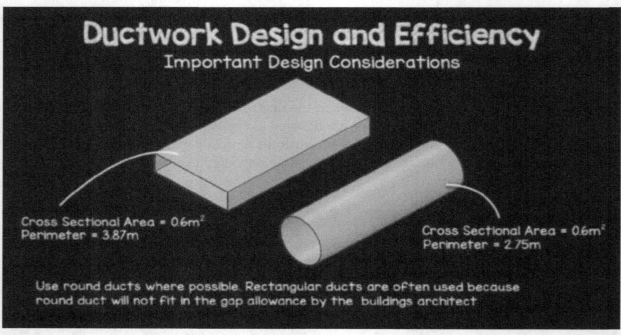

Figure 2.4 Ductwork Design Considerations

Determining Ductwork Requirements: A Technical Perspective

Precision in sizing and selecting ductwork is imperative to achieve exemplary airflow and system performance in HVAC installations. Inadequate or improper sizing may lead to compromised comfort, energy wastage, and escalated operational costs. The calculation of ductwork requirements necessitates a comprehensive understanding of the following key steps:

Load Calculation Methods: Conducting a load calculation constitutes the primary step in assessing the heating and cooling requirements of a space. This calculation accounts for variables such as room dimensions, insulation, occupancy, and heat-emitting equipment. Techniques like the Manual J calculation ascertain the necessary airflow and temperature differentials for the system's smooth operation.

Duct Sizing and Selection: Once the requisite airflow is determined, it is imperative to select an appropriate duct size capable of accommodating the prescribed airflow. The selected duct size should align with the determined air volume and velocity requirements. Diverse sizing methods, including the equal friction method and the velocity reduction method, come into play, considering factors like friction losses, duct material, and system pressure requirements.

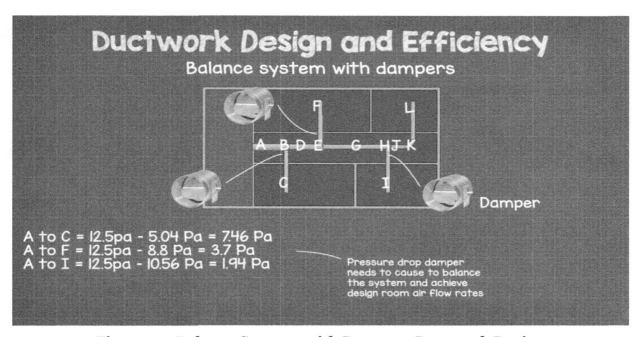

Figure 2.5 Balance Systems with Dampers Ductwork Design

Choice of Duct Material: The material employed in ductwork construction significantly impacts the system's efficiency and durability. Commonly used duct materials comprise galvanized steel, aluminum, and flexible ducting. Each material possesses distinct advantages and considerations, such as cost, weight, insulation properties, and resistance to corrosion. The selection of the suitable duct material hinges on factors like system requirements, budgetary constraints, and compliance with local building codes.

The determination of ductwork requirements involves meticulous consideration of various factors, encompassing airflow volume, velocity, pressure drop, and material selection. It is crucial to recognize that duct sizing represents an iterative process, necessitating adjustments to achieve the desired performance. Consultation of industry guidelines, such as the Air Conditioning Contractors of America (ACCA) Manual D, offers detailed procedures and tables for accurate duct sizing.

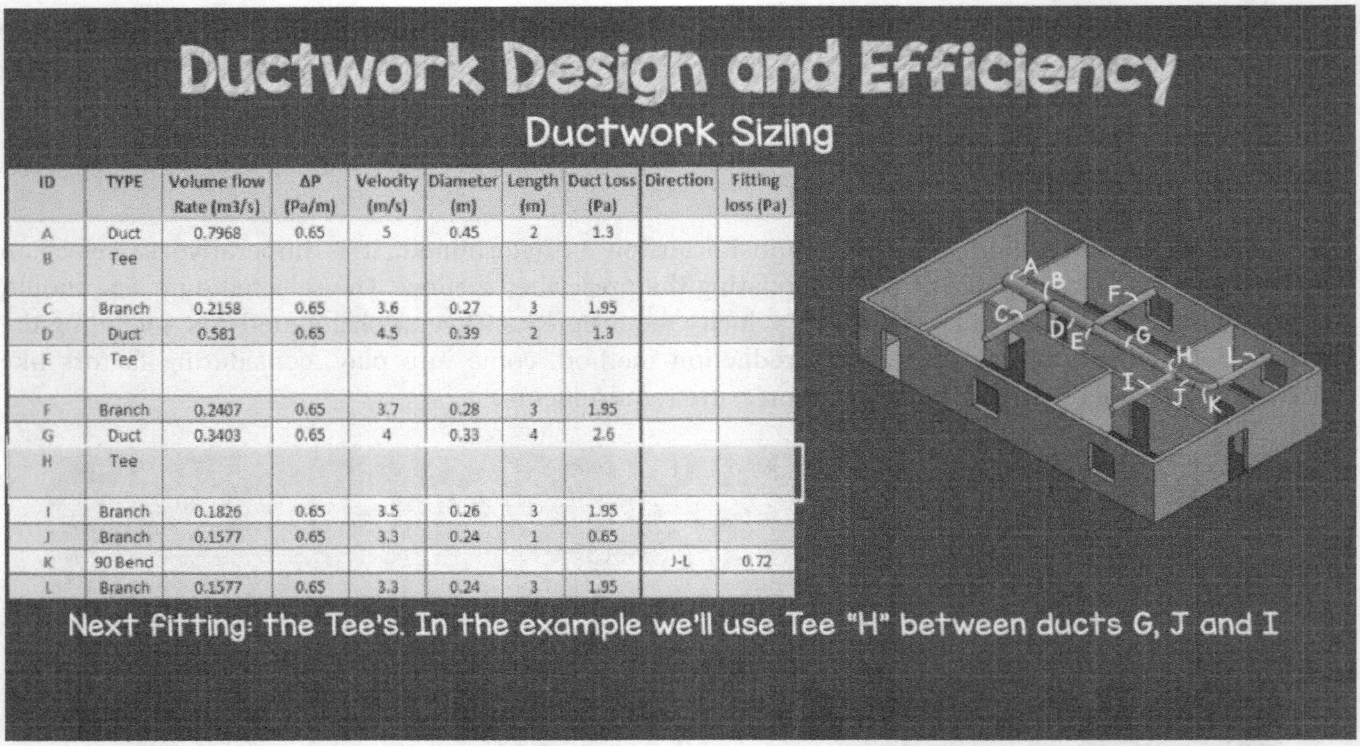

Ductwork Design and Efficiency
Ductwork Sizing

ID	TYPE	Volume flow Rate (m3/s)	ΔP (Pa/m)	Velocity (m/s)	Diameter (m)	Length (m)	Duct Loss (Pa)	Direction	Fitting loss (Pa)
A	Duct	0.7968	0.65	5	0.45	2	1.3		
B	Tee								
C	Branch	0.2158	0.65	3.6	0.27	3	1.95		
D	Duct	0.581	0.65	4.5	0.39	2	1.3		
E	Tee								
F	Branch	0.2407	0.65	3.7	0.28	3	1.95		
G	Duct	0.3403	0.65	4	0.33	4	2.6		
H	Tee								
I	Branch	0.1826	0.65	3.5	0.26	3	1.95		
J	Branch	0.1577	0.65	3.3	0.24	1	0.65		
K	90 Bend							J-L	0.72
L	Branch	0.1577	0.65	3.3	0.24	3	1.95		

Next fitting: the Tee's. In the example we'll use Tee "H" between ducts G, J and I

Figure 2.6 Ductwork Sizing Design Step 1

The layout and design of the ductwork system also warrant careful attention. Deliberate planning of duct routing, branch connections, and fittings serves to minimize pressure losses, ensure even airflow distribution, and obviate potential airflow restrictions. Balancing dampers and airflow measurement devices facilitate system fine-tuning, ensuring the desired airflow in each zone or room.

Properly computed ductwork requirements ensure the efficient distribution of conditioned air, engendering optimal comfort and energy efficiency. For streamlined calculation and precise outcomes, it is advisable to collaborate with experienced HVAC professionals or avail computer software programs exclusively designed for ductwork design.

Ductwork Installation Techniques: A Technical Perspective

A well-executed ductwork installation is indispensable to achieving optimal performance, energy efficiency, and comfort in HVAC systems. The installation process entails a series of techniques and best practices that ensure the duct system functions effectively, efficiently conveying conditioned air. Here are key ductwork installation techniques to consider from a technical standpoint:

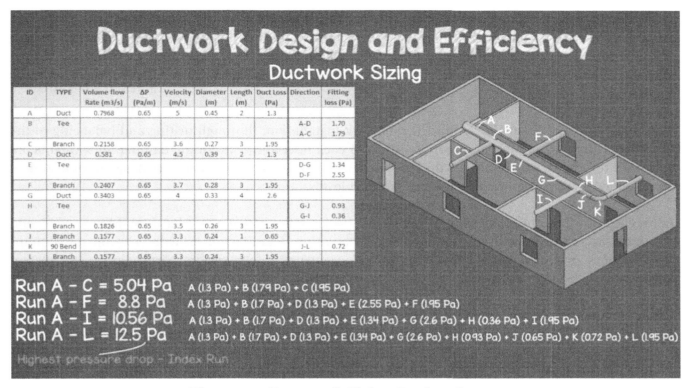

Figure 2.7 Ductwork Sizing Design Step 2

Strategic Planning and Layout Design: Meticulous planning and design of the ductwork layout precede the installation process. Factors like available space, system requirements, and adherence to building codes necessitate thorough consideration. The layout must optimize airflow distribution, minimize pressure losses, and appropriately size ducts and fittings.

Airtight Sealing and Insulation: Ensuring a secure, airtight seal of duct joints and connections is pivotal in preventing air leakage. To this end, suitable sealing materials such as mastic or foil tape must be employed to seal gaps or joints in the ductwork. Insulation plays an integral role, particularly for ducts located in unconditioned spaces, preventing heat gain or loss and preserving desired air temperatures.

Sturdy Support and Fixation: Proper support and fixation of ducts are vital to prevent sagging, vibration, or structural damage over time. Hangers, straps, or brackets must be deployed at regular intervals to ensure adequate support and alignment of the ducts. Excessive bends or kinks, which impede airflow or cause pressure drops, should be avoided.

Mitigate Restrictive Bends and Obstructions: Minimizing the use of sharp bends is critical, as they contribute to increased pressure losses and restricted airflow. Instead, incorporating gradual bends or gentle curves facilitates smooth airflow. Placing ducts away from obstructions like beams or walls ensures unimpeded airflow, minimizing pressure losses.

Precise Sizing and Installation of Registers and Grilles: The installation of supply and return registers and grilles must be executed meticulously, ensuring proper airflow and distribution. Correct sizing and alignment of registers and grilles with the corresponding ducts are paramount. The ability to adjust louvers or dampers permits precise control of airflow direction and volume for individual rooms or zones.

System Testing and Balancing: After the ductwork installation, thorough testing and balancing of the system are imperative. Measurement of airflow in each duct and appropriate damper adjustments are necessary to achieve proper airflow distribution. Balancing the system ensures that each room receives the intended airflow, maintaining optimal comfort levels.

Adherence to Building Codes and Standards: Strict compliance with local building codes and standards is non-negotiable during ductwork installation. Familiarization with relevant regulations, requirements, and guidelines specific to the region ensures safety, system performance, and system longevity.

The execution of proper ductwork installation demands meticulous attention to detail, sound knowledge of HVAC principles, and adherence to best practices. Industry resources, such as guidelines from the Sheet Metal and Air Conditioning Contractors' National Association (SMACNA), offer comprehensive insights into installation techniques and standards.

For individuals lacking expertise in ductwork installation, engaging qualified HVAC professionals is highly recommended. These experts possess the necessary know-how and tools to ensure proper installation, adherence to regulations, and optimization of system performance.

By incorporating these ductwork installation techniques, one can guarantee an HVAC system that operates efficiently, boasts balanced airflow, and consistently delivers optimal comfort throughout the conditioned space.

Selecting the Appropriate HVAC System:

The foremost aspect of HVAC system installation entails the meticulous selection of equipment, a pivotal step in achieving peak performance, energy efficiency, and lasting satisfaction. The chosen HVAC system must precisely align with the building's unique requirements, accounting for variables such as size, climate, occupancy, and budget. Below are the primary considerations in selecting the appropriate HVAC system:

Load Calculation for Heating and Cooling Needs:
Initiate the process by assessing the building's heating and cooling demands. Thoroughly analyze factors such as square footage, insulation levels, occupant count, and heat-producing equipment. Perform a meticulous load calculation to ascertain the system's requisite capacity, factoring in climate, orientation, and heat gain/loss through walls, windows, and roofs.

Prioritize Energy Efficiency:

Efficiency in energy utilization is paramount when selecting an HVAC system. Opt for systems boasting high Annual Fuel Utilization Efficiency (AFUE) and Seasonal Energy Efficiency Ratio (SEER) ratings for furnaces. Energy-efficient technologies significantly reduce energy consumption, minimize utility expenses, and exert a limited environmental impact. Consider exploring intelligent thermostats and energy management systems to further enhance efficiency.

Suitable System Type Selection:
An array of HVAC system types is available, such as heat pumps, split systems, packaged systems, and ductless mini-split systems. Each configuration presents distinct advantages and caveats. Split systems, incorporating indoor and outdoor units, exemplify the most typical and versatile solution. Packaged systems cater to space-constrained environments, housing all components within a single unit. Heat pumps deliver energy-efficient benefits, serving both cooling and heating purposes. Ductless mini-split systems prove ideal for areas lacking ductwork. Assess the merits and drawbacks of each system type based on the building's specific requisites.

Evaluation of Air Distribution Methods:
The method of air distribution is a critical determinant in system selection. Traditional forced-air systems employ ductwork to facilitate conditioned air dispersion. In instances where ductwork is unfeasible or undesirable, alternatives like ductless mini-split systems or radiant heating and cooling systems merit consideration. Thoroughly assess the pros, cons, and installation prerequisites of each air distribution method before finalizing a choice.

Appraisal of Indoor Air Quality (IAQ) Requirements:
Particularly relevant in commercial spaces where occupants spend extended periods, indoor air quality (IAQ) is a critical aspect. Evaluate the building's IAQ needs, encompassing air filtration, humidity regulation, and ventilation systems. Consider incorporating features such as high-efficiency filters, humidity control options, and energy recovery ventilation to optimize indoor air quality.

Consult HVAC Professionals:
Engaging HVAC professionals in the selection process is highly advisable. These experts boast the requisite acumen to evaluate the building's distinct demands, offer counsel on system alternatives, and guarantee compliance with local building codes and regulations. HVAC professionals further facilitate detailed calculations and present cost estimates, empowering an informed decision-making process.

Effective preparation is pivotal to achieving a smooth and successful HVAC system installation. By meticulously preparing the installation site and gathering pertinent information and materials, potential disruptions are minimized, ensuring the installation proceeds efficiently. Crucial preparatory measures encompass:

Assessment of Installation Site Requirements:
Commence by thoroughly evaluating the installation site to identify specific requisites and challenges. Consider aspects such as available space, access points, electrical and plumbing connections, and ventilation demands. A comprehensive analysis of these site-specific details aids in identifying the optimal HVAC equipment placement while anticipating necessary modifications or preparations.

Obtain Essential Permits and Approvals:
In numerous jurisdictions, securing permits and approvals for HVAC system installation is obligatory. Contact the local building department to ascertain permit requirements and any relevant regulations pertaining to HVAC installations. Ensuring all necessary permits are obtained prior to commencing the installation process guarantees compliance with local directives, fostering safety and preempting potential penalties or delays.

Gathering System Specifications and Documentation:
Gather all pertinent documentation and system specifications furnished by the manufacturer or installer. This includes equipment manuals, wiring diagrams, installation instructions, and any warranty particulars. Thoroughly reviewing this documentation ahead of time familiarizes the installer with the system and ensures adherence to the manufacturer's guidelines during installation.

Clearing the Installation Area:
Eliminate any impediments or debris from the installation area. Relocate furniture, equipment, or belongings that might hinder access to the installation site. By establishing a clean and unobstructed workspace, HVAC technicians can work efficiently and safely.

Verifying Proper Electrical and Plumbing Connections:
Confirm that the required electrical and plumbing connections for the HVAC system are duly in place and functioning effectively. In instances where modifications or upgrades are necessary, enlist the services of qualified professionals to ensure compliance with electrical and plumbing codes. Suitable connections are vital to the secure and efficient operation of the HVAC system.

Coordination with Other Trades:
If the HVAC system installation is a component of a larger construction or renovation project, coordinate with the other trades involved. This includes electricians, plumbers, and construction crews. Assure the timely availability of necessary infrastructure, such as electrical panels, ductwork, and piping, compatible with the HVAC system installation.

Effective communication with the HVAC installer throughout the preparation phase is essential. Address specific requirements or concerns, such as access restrictions, scheduling considerations, or equipment delivery arrangements. By maintaining clear and timely communication, potential issues are readily addressed, ensuring a seamless installation experience.

Comprehensive understanding of the HVAC equipment installation process and adherence to specific procedures are fundamental in ensuring proper functionality, efficiency, and safety. Whether installing a furnace, air conditioner, heat pump, or any other HVAC component, meticulous adherence to the following essential steps results in a successful installation:

Prioritize Safety Precautions:
Safety takes precedence before commencing any installation work. Ensuring that the equipment's power supply is turned off and implementing necessary measures to prevent electrical shocks are imperative. Personal protective equipment (PPE) such as gloves and safety glasses should be donned

when handling equipment and working with tools. Complying with manufacturer safety guidelines and local safety regulations is vital.

Equipment Positioning:
Carefully position the HVAC equipment in the designated installation area, considering site requirements, clearances, and service access. Ensure that the equipment is leveled and securely stabilized, utilizing appropriate supports or mounting brackets as warranted. Noise reduction and vibration isolation measures may be applied to minimize disturbances arising from the equipment.

Electrical Connections:
Secure and efficient operation of HVAC equipment hinges on accurate electrical connections. Follow the manufacturer's instructions and electrical diagrams meticulously to establish connections to the power supply. Verify that all electrical connections are firmly secured and adequately insulated. Conduct voltage and amperage checks to validate the functionality of electrical connections.

Refrigerant Lines and Plumbing Connections:
For HVAC equipment involving refrigerant lines or plumbing connections, meticulously install and connect these elements in accordance with manufacturer guidelines. Ensure proper sizing, insulation, and sealing of refrigerant lines to obviate leaks and uphold system efficiency. Follow plumbing codes and guidelines during water line connections, drains, or condensate lines.

Ductwork Installation:
Should the HVAC system entail ductwork, follow the predetermined layout and design for duct installation. Ensure the appropriate sizing and sealing of ducts to minimize air leakage. Utilize suitable fasteners and supports to secure the ductwork, taking care to avoid excessive bends or restrictions that could impede airflow. Install dampers, registers, and grilles following manufacturer guidelines.

Ventilation and Exhaust Systems:
When the HVAC equipment encompasses ventilation or exhaust systems, ensure their correct installation and connection. Comply with ventilation guidelines to facilitate adequate fresh air intake and proper ventilation of combustion gases, if applicable. Install exhaust fans or vents according to local codes and manufacturer recommendations.

System Start-up and Testing:
Upon completing the installation, initiate system start-up procedures and conduct comprehensive testing. Verify that the equipment starts and operates accurately, scrutinizing for abnormal noises, vibrations, or malfunctions. Test airflow, temperature differentials, and system pressures, ensuring they adhere to manufacturer specifications. Make adjustments as necessary to optimize system performance.

Documentation and User Instructions:
Document all installation details, including equipment specifications, electrical and plumbing connections, ductwork layout, and any adjustments or modifications executed during installation. Provide comprehensive user instructions on HVAC system operation, encompassing routine maintenance procedures and safety considerations.

Preventive Maintenance for HVAC Systems

Importance of Regular Maintenance

Regular maintenance is crucial for the optimal performance, efficiency, and longevity of HVAC systems. Neglecting routine maintenance can lead to reduced system efficiency, increased energy consumption, costly repairs, and premature equipment failure. By prioritizing preventive maintenance, you can enjoy several important benefits for your HVAC system and overall comfort. Here are some key reasons why regular maintenance is essential:

HVAC
PREVENTATIVE MAINTENANCE STRATEGIES

1. **Filter Replacement**
2. **Coil Cleaning**
3. **Water Treatment & Glycol Level**
4. **Exercising Valves**
5. **Flushing Strainers**
6. **Cleaning Cooling Towers**

Figure 2.8 Importance of Regular Maintenance

Improved Energy Efficiency:

HVAC systems that receive regular maintenance operate more efficiently. Over time, dust, debris, and dirt can accumulate on critical components such as coils, filters, and fans, reducing system airflow and heat transfer. This buildup forces the system to work harder, consuming more energy to achieve the desired temperature levels. Regular maintenance, including cleaning and replacing filters, inspecting and cleaning coils, and optimizing airflow, ensures that the system operates at its peak efficiency, minimizing energy waste and lowering utility bills.

Extended Equipment Lifespan:

To get the most value out of your investment in HVAC systems, it is crucial to extend their lives. Regular maintenance assists in spotting and resolving minor issues before they become more serious ones that could result in equipment failure. You may minimize component wear and tear, increase the equipment's lifespan, and postpone the need for expensive replacements by maintaining the system clean, greased, and properly adjusted.

Enhanced Indoor Air Quality:

Maintaining indoor air quality (IAQ) requires the use of HVAC systems. The inhabitants' health and comfort might be negatively impacted by dust, allergies, and other airborne contaminants that can build up in the system and circulate throughout the building. Regular maintenance contributes to better IAQ by cleaning or changing air filters, examining and cleaning ductwork, and making sure

36

there is adequate ventilation. Healthy indoor settings are supported by clean filters and properly maintained components that assist filter out pollutants, allergens, and particles from the air.

Prevention of Costly Breakdowns:
Regular maintenance helps identify and address potential issues before they lead to system breakdowns. During maintenance visits, HVAC technicians can identify worn-out components, loose electrical connections, refrigerant leaks, or other signs of malfunction. Timely detection and repair of these issues can prevent costly breakdowns, emergency repairs, and inconvenience. By proactively addressing maintenance needs, you can minimize downtime, increase system reliability, and avoid unexpected expenses.

Optimal Comfort Levels:
A well-maintained HVAC system delivers consistent and reliable comfort throughout the conditioned space. Regular maintenance ensures that the system is capable of maintaining the desired temperature and humidity levels. Components such as thermostats, sensors, and control systems are inspected and calibrated to ensure accurate and responsive operation. By maintaining optimal comfort levels, you enhance occupant satisfaction, productivity, and overall well-being.

Compliance with Warranty Requirements:
HVAC manufacturers often require regular maintenance as a condition for maintaining warranty coverage. Failure to perform routine maintenance as recommended by the manufacturer can void warranty protection. Adhering to maintenance requirements helps protect your investment and ensures that you can rely on warranty coverage should any major issues arise.

To reap the benefits of regular maintenance, it's advisable to establish a maintenance schedule and work with qualified HVAC professionals. They have the expertise to perform comprehensive system inspections, cleaning, lubrication, and adjustment tasks. HVAC professionals can also provide personalized recommendations based on the specific needs of your system and help you stay on top of maintenance requirements.

HVAC Maintenance Checklist
Implementing a comprehensive HVAC maintenance checklist is crucial to ensure the proper functioning, efficiency, and longevity of your heating, ventilation, and air conditioning system. Regular maintenance helps identify potential issues, prevent costly breakdowns, and optimize system performance. While specific maintenance requirements may vary depending on the type of HVAC system and manufacturer recommendations, here are some essential tasks to include in your HVAC maintenance checklist:

Regular Filter Inspection and Replacement: Inspect air filters on a monthly basis and replace them as needed, typically every one to three months. Clogged or dirty filters restrict airflow, reduce system efficiency, and can lead to issues such as frozen coils or overheating. Follow the manufacturer's guidelines for the correct filter type and replacement schedule.

Cleaning of Condenser and Evaporator Coils: Over time, dirt, debris, and dust can accumulate on the condenser and evaporator coils, hindering heat transfer and reducing system efficiency. Clean the coils annually or as recommended by the manufacturer. Use coil cleaning solutions, a soft brush, or a specialized coil cleaning tool to remove the buildup and improve heat exchange.

Inspection and Cleaning of Fan Blades: Inspect the fan blades for any dirt or debris accumulation. Clean the blades and ensure they are balanced and properly aligned. Misaligned or unbalanced blades can cause vibrations and put additional stress on the motor.

Lubrication of Moving Parts: Lubricate motor bearings, fan motors, and other moving parts as per the manufacturer's recommendations. Proper lubrication reduces friction, extends the life of the components, and ensures smooth operation.

Inspection and Cleaning of Ductwork: Regularly inspect the ductwork for leaks, loose connections, or signs of damage. Seal any leaks or gaps to prevent air loss and maintain system efficiency. Clean the ductwork periodically to remove dust, debris, and potential allergens that can affect indoor air quality.

Calibration of Thermostats and Controls: Check the accuracy and calibration of thermostats and controls. Verify that temperature sensors are functioning correctly and that the system responds accurately to the desired settings. Calibrate thermostats if necessary to ensure accurate temperature control.

Testing and Calibration of Safety Controls: Test and calibrate safety controls such as high-pressure switches, limit switches, and flame sensors. Ensure that these controls are functioning properly to protect the system from potential malfunctions or safety hazards.

Inspection of Electrical Connections: Regularly inspect electrical connections, terminals, and wiring for signs of damage, loose connections, or corrosion. Tighten loose connections and address any electrical issues promptly to prevent safety hazards.

Checking Refrigerant Levels: Verify refrigerant levels and ensure they are within the manufacturer's specified range. Low refrigerant levels can indicate a leak or other issues that need to be addressed promptly to maintain system performance.

Examination of Belts and Pulleys: Inspect belts for signs of wear, cracks, or damage. Replace worn-out belts and ensure proper tension. Check pulleys for alignment and wear. Misaligned belts or damaged pulleys can cause excessive strain on the system and lead to premature failure.

Cleaning and Maintenance of Outdoor Units: Remove any debris, leaves, or vegetation from the outdoor unit. Trim any nearby foliage to ensure proper airflow. Inspect the unit for damage and clean it using a hose or soft brush.

Verification of System Performance: Monitor the system's overall performance, including temperature differentials, airflow, and system pressures. Measure and record these parameters periodically to detect any variations or abnormalities that may indicate underlying issues.

Scheduling and Planning Maintenance Tasks

Properly scheduling and planning maintenance tasks for your HVAC system is essential for ensuring its optimal performance, longevity, and energy efficiency. By following a structured approach, you can effectively manage maintenance activities and stay on top of routine tasks. Here are some important considerations for scheduling and planning HVAC system maintenance:

Create a Maintenance Calendar:

Establish a maintenance calendar that outlines the frequency of various tasks. Consider manufacturer recommendations, industry best practices, and your specific system's requirements. Note the recommended intervals for tasks such as filter replacements, coil cleanings, inspections, and calibration. A calendar helps you track upcoming maintenance needs and ensures that tasks are performed at the appropriate times.

Prioritize Preventive Maintenance:

Prioritize preventative maintenance actions that assist in identifying and resolving possible issues before they develop into significant concerns. This entails routine calibration, cleaning, lubrication, and inspections. In addition to enhancing system efficiency, preventive maintenance lowers the possibility of unanticipated failures and exorbitant repairs.

Consider Seasonal Demands:

HVAC systems often have different maintenance requirements based on seasonal demands. For example, in the fall, you may need to focus on heating system maintenance, while in the spring, air conditioning maintenance takes precedence. Adjust your maintenance calendar to align with seasonal needs and ensure that the appropriate tasks are performed at the right time.

Account for System Usage and Conditions:

The usage patterns and environmental conditions in your specific location can affect the maintenance needs of your HVAC system. Systems in high-use environments or areas with significant dust, pollen, or other contaminants may require more frequent filter replacements and coil cleanings. Take these factors into account when planning maintenance tasks and adjust your schedule accordingly.

Allocate Sufficient Time and Resources:

Ensure that you allocate sufficient time and resources for performing maintenance tasks. Some tasks may require more time or specialized equipment. Plan ahead and allocate the necessary resources, whether it's scheduling dedicated maintenance personnel or arranging for external HVAC professionals to perform more complex tasks.

Document and Track Maintenance Activities:

Keep thorough records of all maintenance procedures, including dates, tasks completed, and any conclusions or advice. With the use of this paperwork, you can keep track of the maintenance that has been performed on your HVAC system, spot patterns or reoccurring problems, and use it as a guide for future maintenance planning. It also helps with warranty compliance and is a useful tool for system optimization and troubleshooting.

Consider Professional Assistance:
While some maintenance tasks can be performed by homeowners, certain procedures require the expertise of HVAC professionals. Consider scheduling annual or bi-annual maintenance visits with qualified technicians who can perform comprehensive inspections, servicing, and fine-tuning. Their expertise ensures that all maintenance tasks are performed correctly and in accordance with manufacturer recommendations and industry standards.

Stay Informed and Updated:
Stay informed about the latest industry developments, technological advancements, and manufacturer guidelines. HVAC systems evolve over time, and new maintenance practices may emerge. Regularly review and update your maintenance plan to incorporate any relevant changes or recommendations.

How To Check Amp Draws
Checking amp draws is a crucial task in HVAC maintenance and troubleshooting. It helps ensure the efficient and safe operation of electrical components in the system. To check amp draws, follow these steps:

Gather Necessary Equipment: You'll need a digital multimeter capable of measuring AC amps. Make sure the meter is rated for the maximum amp load of the HVAC system.

Turn off Power: Before starting, turn off the power supply to the HVAC unit at the breaker or disconnect switch to avoid electrical hazards.

Access Electrical Components: Gain access to the electrical components you want to test. This may involve removing panels or covers to reach the wires.

Connect the Multimeter: Set the multimeter to measure AC amps and connect the meter leads in series with the electrical component you're testing. For example, to measure the amp draw of a compressor, place one lead on the incoming power wire and the other lead on the wire connected to the compressor.

Restore Power and Monitor: Once the multimeter is properly connected, restore power to the HVAC unit. Observe the amp reading on the multimeter while the component is running. Take multiple readings to ensure accuracy.

Compare with Manufacturer Specifications: Compare the amp draw readings to the manufacturer's specifications. Most electrical components have a rated amp draw, and the measured value should be within a certain tolerance range of this rating.

Troubleshoot if Necessary: If the amp draw is significantly higher or lower than the manufacturer's specifications, it may indicate an issue with the component or the system. Consult the HVAC system's documentation or seek the help of a professional technician for further troubleshooting and repairs.

Turn off Power and Disconnect: After completing the amp draw measurement, turn off the power again and disconnect the multimeter from the electrical components.

Regularly checking amp draws of electrical components in the HVAC system can help identify potential problems, prevent breakdowns, and optimize energy efficiency. Always prioritize safety and consider seeking assistance from a qualified HVAC technician for complex issues.

Troubleshooting Common HVAC Problems

HVAC systems, being intricate mechanical systems, are susceptible to occasional malfunctions, akin to any machinery. A thorough grasp of common HVAC issues and their remedies empowers one to execute preliminary troubleshooting or discern the need for professional intervention. Herein, we delineate prevalent HVAC predicaments and their potential resolutions:

Insufficient Heating or Cooling:
Inadequate heating or cooling may arise from an array of factors. Initial scrutiny of thermostat settings, calibrated precisely to the desired temperature, is crucial. Persisting discrepancies may emanate from obstructed air filters hampering airflow, a malfunctioning thermostat, a defective compressor, or refrigerant leaks. Routinely cleanse or replace air filters and contemplate soliciting professional aid for more intricate quandaries.

Uneven Heating or Cooling:
Non-uniform temperature distribution within a space stems from diverse causes. Blocked vents or registers, improperly sized ductwork, or imbalanced airflow may be the culprits. Verify the openness and unobstructed state of all vents and registers. Should the aberration persist, enlist a professional's expertise to scrutinize your ductwork for design or installation irregularities responsible for the imbalance.

HVAC System Frequent Cycling:
Frequent cycling of the HVAC system betrays an underlying quandary. The root causes may encompass clogged air filters, erroneous thermostat settings, a malfunctioning blower motor, or electrical component malfunctions. Initially, inspect and replace the air filter if necessitated. In the event of unresolved issues, seek expert consultation for meticulous diagnosis and remediation.

Aberrant Noises:
Unconventional noises originating from the HVAC system signify underlying issues. Rattling, grinding, or squealing sounds may indicate loose or worn-out components, such as fan blades, bearings, or belts. Hissing or gurgling sounds may denote refrigerant leaks. Discerning peculiar noises warrants professional attention, averting aggravated system afflictions.

Impaired Air Quality:
Detrimental indoor air quality adversely affects comfort and health. HVAC systems might circulate dust, allergens, and pollutants throughout living spaces. Routine air filter maintenance or replacement and the acquisition of supplementary air filtration or purification systems are prudent measures. Adequate ventilation and regular HVAC system maintenance also foster improved indoor air quality.

Escalated Energy Consumption:

Significantly elevated energy bills may be attributable to an inefficient HVAC system. The contributing factors could encompass soiled air filters, obstructed ductwork, refrigerant leaks, or malfunctioning components. Methodical system maintenance, encompassing air filter, coil, and ductwork cleaning, is paramount. Intransigent circumstances necessitate consultation with an HVAC professional for efficacy assessment and suitable solutions.

System Non-Operational:

System failure to initiate operation may be ascribed to diverse etiologies. Verification of the power supply, circuit breakers, and switches for appropriate functioning is requisite. In the event of continued non-operation, potential causes may entail a faulty thermostat, a malfunctioning motor, or electrical aberrations. Such predicaments necessitate the engagement of adept technicians for diagnosis and redress.

Refrigerant Leaks:

Low refrigerant levels can compromise HVAC system functioning, resulting in subpar cooling performance. Suspecting refrigerant leakage mandates prompt involvement of a professional HVAC technician to ascertain and rectify the leak. Mere addition of refrigerant sans addressing the leakage is a stopgap measure and augments potential damage to the system.

Remembrance that while rudimentary troubleshooting may address certain HVAC issues, proficient intervention is indispensable for others. In situations of uncertainty regarding diagnosis or resolution, professional guidance is prudent. Regular maintenance and timely resolution of HVAC predicaments guarantee optimal system performance, energy efficiency, and abiding comfort within the residential or occupational setting.

Book 3

Ventilation Systems

Importance of Ventilation in HVAC Systems

The Role of Ventilation in Indoor Air Quality

Ventilation is crucial in the world of heating, ventilation, and air conditioning (HVAC) systems for providing high-quality indoor air. The quality and freshness of the air we breathe indoors is directly impacted by ventilation, despite the fact that temperature control and humidity regulation are significant parts of HVAC. Anyone looking to master HVAC systems must comprehend the significance ventilation plays in indoor air quality.

Ventilation serves two primary purposes when it comes to indoor air quality: dilution and removal of pollutants. It achieves this by introducing fresh outdoor air and expelling stale air from within a building. Here are some key points to consider regarding the role of ventilation in indoor air quality:

Removal of Indoor Pollutants:

Volatile organic compounds (VOCs), scents, allergies, and contaminants generated by building materials, furniture, cleaning supplies, and human activities are just a few of the pollutants that can be found in indoor spaces. By circulating interior air with clean outdoor air, ventilation lowers the quantity of harmful contaminants while enhancing overall air quality.

Moisture and Humidity Control:

Proper ventilation aids in controlling moisture levels and mitigating excessive humidity. Excessive moisture can lead to mold growth, musty odors, and increased risk of respiratory issues. By introducing fresh air and exhausting humid air, ventilation helps to maintain optimal humidity levels, preventing the accumulation of excess moisture and mold-related problems.

Removal of Stale Air and Odors:

Over time, indoor spaces can accumulate stale air, particularly in areas with poor ventilation. Stale air can be uncomfortable and lead to unpleasant odors. Ventilation systems facilitate the removal of stale air, ensuring a constant supply of fresh air and promoting a more pleasant and inviting indoor environment.

Provision of Adequate Oxygen:

Ventilation replenishes the oxygen levels within indoor spaces. Sufficient oxygen is vital for human health and cognitive function. In spaces with inadequate ventilation, oxygen levels can decrease, leading to feelings of drowsiness, reduced concentration, and discomfort. Proper ventilation ensures an ample supply of oxygen, contributing to improved overall well-being and productivity.

Reduction of Indoor Airborne Contaminants:

In addition to removing specific pollutants, ventilation helps to reduce the concentration of airborne contaminants, such as dust, pet dander, and pollen. By continuously exchanging indoor air with fresh outdoor air, ventilation systems help to filter out and dilute these particles, promoting cleaner and healthier indoor air.

Understanding the crucial role of ventilation in maintaining indoor air quality emphasizes the need for well-designed and properly functioning ventilation systems within HVAC setups. By effectively removing pollutants, controlling moisture levels, eliminating odors, and providing adequate oxygen, ventilation plays a vital role in creating a comfortable and healthy indoor environment.

Health and Comfort Benefits of Proper Ventilation

Proper ventilation is not only essential for maintaining good indoor air quality, but it also offers a range of health and comfort benefits. When HVAC systems incorporate effective ventilation strategies, occupants can experience improved well-being, enhanced comfort levels, and a reduced risk of certain health issues. Understanding the health and comfort benefits of proper ventilation is crucial in recognizing its significance within HVAC systems.

Removal of Indoor Air Pollutants:

Removal of indoor air contaminants is one of the main health advantages of effective ventilation. VOCs, particulate matter, allergens, and chemical contaminants are just a few of the pollutants that can be found indoors. Without sufficient ventilation, these pollutants can build up and cause long-term health hazards, allergic reactions, asthmatic flare-ups, and respiratory irritation. In order to improve overall indoor air quality and protect inhabitants' health, proper ventilation aids in the dilution and removal of harmful pollutants.

Prevention of Mold and Moisture-Related Issues:

Insufficient ventilation can contribute to excess moisture accumulation, creating a favorable environment for mold growth. Mold not only affects the structural integrity of buildings but can also trigger allergic reactions, respiratory problems, and other health issues. Proper ventilation, combined with moisture control measures, helps to minimize excess humidity and prevent mold growth, thus promoting a healthier indoor environment.

Regulation of Indoor Temperature and Comfort:

Ventilation systems play a vital role in regulating indoor temperature and enhancing occupant comfort. By introducing fresh air and removing heat generated by occupants, appliances, and sunlight, ventilation helps to prevent stuffiness and maintain a comfortable environment. In addition, effective ventilation can reduce the perception of odors and control the spread of airborne contaminants, creating a more pleasant and enjoyable indoor space.

Provision of Adequate Oxygen Supply:

Proper ventilation ensures a sufficient supply of fresh outdoor air, which contains a higher oxygen concentration than indoor air. Sufficient oxygen levels are essential for maintaining optimal cognitive function, alertness, and overall well-being. Inadequate ventilation can lead to feelings of drowsiness, reduced productivity, and discomfort due to a lack of oxygen. By introducing fresh air, ventilation systems help to replenish oxygen levels, promoting a healthier and more energized indoor environment.

Enhanced Mental and Psychological Well-being:

Good indoor air quality, achieved through proper ventilation, has been linked to improved mental and psychological well-being. Research suggests that exposure to poor indoor air quality, including elevated levels of pollutants and inadequate ventilation, can contribute to symptoms such as fatigue, irritability, difficulty concentrating, and increased stress levels. On the other hand, a well-ventilated environment with clean and fresh air can positively impact mood, cognitive performance, and overall mental health.

By recognizing and implementing proper ventilation practices, HVAC systems can provide significant health and comfort benefits for occupants. Through the removal of indoor pollutants, prevention of mold and moisture-related issues, regulation of indoor temperature, provision of adequate oxygen, and enhancement of mental well-being, ventilation contributes to creating a healthier, more comfortable, and pleasant indoor environment.

Energy Efficiency and Ventilation
When it comes to HVAC systems, energy efficiency is a critical consideration. While ventilation plays a vital role in maintaining good indoor air quality and occupant comfort, it is also essential to balance the energy requirements of ventilation with overall system efficiency. Understanding the relationship between energy efficiency and ventilation is crucial for optimizing HVAC performance and reducing energy consumption.

Demand-Controlled Ventilation:
Demand-Controlled Ventilation (DCV) is a resource-saving technique that modifies the ventilation rate in response to occupancy and pollution levels in real time. DCV systems adjust the airflow rather than running at a constant ventilation rate to suit the unique requirements of the space. With this strategy, ventilation is delivered when and where it is required, preventing energy waste from over-ventilating vacant or lightly populated spaces. DCV systems can optimize energy economy without sacrificing indoor air quality by integrating occupancy sensors, carbon dioxide (CO_2) sensors, or other pollution detectors.

Energy Recovery Ventilation:
Another method for improving the energy efficiency of ventilation systems is energy recovery ventilation (ERV). The heat or coolness is transferred to the incoming fresh air by ERV systems from the exhaust air stream. The energy needed to condition the incoming air is decreased by this process, which enables the exchange of heat or energy between the outgoing and incoming air streams. ERV systems precool incoming hot air using the coolness of the exhaust air during cooling seasons and preheat arriving cold air using the heat from the exhaust air during heating seasons. ERV systems lead to significant energy savings while maintaining acceptable ventilation rates by recovering and recycling energy.

Proper Ventilation System Design:
Effective ventilation system design can significantly impact energy efficiency. By considering factors such as duct layout, air distribution, and sizing, designers can optimize airflow patterns, minimize pressure losses, and reduce the energy required to distribute air throughout a building. Properly sized and designed ventilation systems ensure that air is delivered efficiently to each space, minimizing energy waste associated with fan power consumption and excessive ductwork losses. Additionally, well-designed systems can mitigate issues such as air leakage and unbalanced airflow, further enhancing energy efficiency.

Integrated HVAC Controls:
Integrating ventilation controls with other HVAC components and controls can lead to improved energy efficiency. By synchronizing the operation of ventilation systems with heating and cooling equipment, occupant schedules, and occupancy sensing, energy consumption can be optimized. For example, linking the operation of ventilation fans to the operation of heating or cooling systems ensures that ventilation is provided only when necessary, avoiding unnecessary energy consumption during unoccupied periods.

Regular Maintenance and Filter Replacement:
Proper maintenance of ventilation systems is crucial for preserving energy efficiency. Regular cleaning and inspection of ventilation components, such as fans, ductwork, and filters, help maintain optimal system performance. Clogged or dirty filters restrict airflow, increasing the energy required for ventilation. By adhering to a scheduled maintenance plan and replacing filters as recommended by manufacturers, the system can operate at its highest efficiency, ensuring effective ventilation while minimizing energy usage.

Types of Ventilation Systems

Natural Ventilation:
Natural ventilation is a passive ventilation strategy that exploits external air currents and temperature differences to achieve indoor air renewal and thermal comfort without reliance on mechanical aids. The essence of natural ventilation lies in the exchange of air between indoor and outdoor environments, facilitated by natural phenomena such as wind, the stack effect, and buoyancy. Harnessing these forces entails strategically situating openings, such as windows, vents, or louvers, to promote continuous airflow.
Design Considerations:
Designing for natural ventilation necessitates meticulous deliberation on factors such as building orientation, site conditions, climate, internal layout, and occupant requirements. Salient design considerations encompass the positioning and sizing of openings, the establishment of unobstructed airflow paths, the incorporation of adjustable elements for occupant control, and the optimization of cross-ventilation for enhanced efficiency.

Pros and Cons:
Natural ventilation offers notable advantages in HVAC systems, including energy efficiency, sustainable attributes, direct outdoor air supply, cost-effectiveness, and a heightened connection to nature. However, its efficacy is contingent on climatic conditions and is subject to reduced control over indoor conditions, potential noise penetration, and security vulnerabilities inherent in exposed openings.

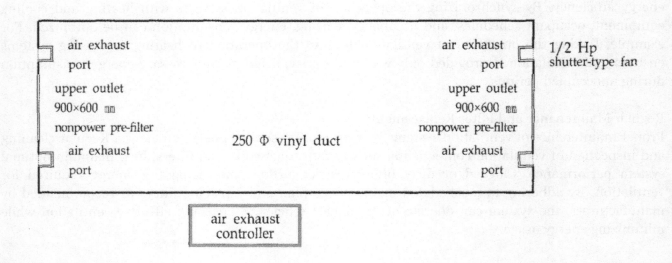

Figure 3.1 Air Exhaust Controller

Mechanical Ventilation:

Mechanical ventilation is an active ventilation approach that employs mechanical equipment, such as fans, blowers, and ductwork, to effectuate controlled airflow within a building. Unlike natural ventilation, mechanical ventilation facilitates precise regulation of ventilation rates, air distribution, and pressure differentials. It represents a prevalent and versatile method in HVAC systems, catering to diverse building typologies and occupant demands.

Principles:

Operating on the principle of forced air movement, mechanical ventilation employs mechanical devices to introduce outdoor air, exhaust stale air, or achieve a balanced exchange to maintain indoor air quality and occupant comfort. Fans, blowers, dampers, and ductwork orchestrate controlled airflow and pressure differentials, enabling fine-grained regulation of ventilation.

Types of Mechanical Ventilation Systems:

Mechanical ventilation encompasses various configurations tailored to distinct requirements:

Exhaust Ventilation: This system focuses on expelling contaminants and stale air from specific rooms, such as restrooms and kitchens. Exhaust blowers facilitate the removal of air, typically vented to the outdoors.

Supply Ventilation: Supply ventilation systems introduce fresh outdoor air to indoor spaces, either directly or through a network of ducts and diffusers. Incoming air replaces the exhausted air, preserving balanced airflow and avoiding negative pressurization.

Balanced Ventilation: Combining elements of both exhaust and supply systems, balanced ventilation seeks equilibrium by simultaneously introducing fresh air and expelling stale air, ensuring balanced airflow throughout the building.

Heat Recovery Ventilation (HRV)/Energy Recovery Ventilation (ERV): HRV and ERV systems recover heat or cooling from exhaust air, transferring thermal energy to the incoming fresh air. Heat exchangers facilitate the energy transfer, resulting in enhanced ventilation efficiency and energy conservation.

Benefits:
Mechanical ventilation systems offer various advantages that render them favorable in HVAC applications. These encompass precise control over airflow and air quality, adaptability to diverse building scenarios, improved indoor air quality, flexibility for integration with other HVAC components, and compliance with building codes mandating adequate ventilation and safety.

Exhaust Ventilation:
Exhaust ventilation focuses on the efficient removal of contaminants and stale air from specific areas in a building. It relies on dedicated exhaust blowers to draw air from spaces where pollutants are generated, such as kitchens, bathrooms, laboratories, or industrial settings. The exhaust air is expelled to the outdoors, ensuring a continuous supply of fresh air. Exhaust ventilation systems are essential in spaces where airborne contaminants need to be swiftly removed to maintain a healthy and safe indoor environment.

Design Considerations:
Designing an effective exhaust ventilation system requires careful consideration of the location and size of exhaust points, the ventilation rates, and the coordination with supply ventilation to achieve proper airflow balance. Determining the appropriate exhaust fan capacity based on the specific requirements of each space is crucial to ensure efficient contaminant removal and maintain adequate air quality.

Pros and Cons:
Exhaust ventilation systems offer the advantage of targeted pollutant removal, preventing the buildup of harmful substances in specific areas. They are particularly useful in spaces where a continuous influx of fresh air may not be necessary, such as restrooms or kitchens. However, they may lead to negative pressure in the building if not correctly balanced with supply ventilation. Additionally, exhaust ventilation relies on mechanical equipment, which can consume energy and require regular maintenance.

Supply Ventilation:
Supply ventilation is focused on providing fresh outdoor air to the building's occupied spaces. The system introduces outdoor air directly or through ductwork and distributes it throughout the building, replacing the exhausted air. The controlled supply of fresh air helps maintain balanced air pressure and ensures adequate ventilation to meet occupant comfort and air quality requirements.

Design Considerations:
In designing supply ventilation systems, considerations include the calculation of the required outdoor air intake rate, the proper distribution of air throughout the building, and the control mechanisms for adjusting airflow rates based on occupancy and environmental conditions. Balancing supply and

exhaust ventilation is crucial to prevent negative pressure, which can cause infiltration of outdoor pollutants and affect the indoor environment.

Pros and Cons:
Supply ventilation systems offer the benefit of ensuring a continuous supply of fresh outdoor air, which is essential for maintaining indoor air quality and creating a healthy living or working environment. These systems can be efficiently controlled to meet specific occupancy needs and respond to changing environmental conditions. However, supply ventilation may not be sufficient on its own to remove indoor pollutants, as it relies on exhaust ventilation or natural air leakage to remove stale air and contaminants.

Balanced Ventilation:
Balanced ventilation systems aim to achieve equilibrium between supply and exhaust ventilation. These systems incorporate both supply and exhaust components to ensure a balanced exchange of indoor and outdoor air. By simultaneously introducing fresh air and expelling stale air, balanced ventilation systems maintain a stable indoor environment with optimal air quality and comfort.
Design Considerations:
Designing balanced ventilation systems involves careful attention to the airflow rates of both supply and exhaust components. The goal is to ensure that the amount of outdoor air brought in is equal to the amount of air exhausted, preventing pressure imbalances and maintaining a consistent indoor environment. To achieve this balance, the design must consider the occupancy levels, indoor air quality requirements, and the outdoor air conditions.

Pros and Cons:
The main advantage of balanced ventilation systems is their ability to provide consistent and controlled airflow, promoting a healthy indoor environment without causing negative pressure or excessive energy consumption. These systems are particularly well-suited for tightly sealed buildings, where natural ventilation may not be sufficient. However, balanced ventilation systems typically require mechanical equipment, and their design and installation can be more complex compared to other ventilation strategies.

Heat Recovery Ventilation (HRV) and Energy Recovery Ventilation (ERV):
HRV and ERV systems are advanced ventilation technologies that enhance energy efficiency by recovering thermal energy from exhaust air and transferring it to the incoming fresh air. These systems use heat exchangers to exchange energy between the two air streams, minimizing the energy needed to condition the incoming air. HRV systems transfer heat only, while ERV systems transfer both heat and moisture, making them ideal for humid climates.
Design Considerations:
Designing HRV and ERV systems requires careful selection of the appropriate heat exchanger type, sizing, and efficiency. The design should also consider the air distribution, pressure differentials, and control mechanisms to ensure optimal energy recovery and ventilation performance.

Pros and Cons:
HRV and ERV systems offer significant energy savings by reducing the heating or cooling load required to condition incoming air. By pre-conditioning the fresh air, these systems enhance indoor

comfort and reduce energy consumption. However, the installation and maintenance of HRV and ERV systems may require a higher initial investment, and their efficiency depends on climate conditions and usage patterns.

Understanding the various types of ventilation systems, including their principles, design considerations, and benefits, is crucial for HVAC professionals to select the most appropriate system for each building's specific needs. Properly designed and implemented ventilation systems play a fundamental role in creating healthy, comfortable, and energy-efficient indoor environments.

Components and Design Considerations for Ventilation

Heat Recovery Ventilation (HRV) and Energy Recovery Ventilation (ERV):
HRV and ERV systems are advanced ventilation technologies that aim to enhance energy efficiency and indoor comfort. These systems incorporate heat exchangers to recover thermal energy from exhaust air and transfer it to the incoming fresh air. HRV systems focus on transferring heat, while ERV systems also transfer moisture, making them particularly suitable for humid climates.

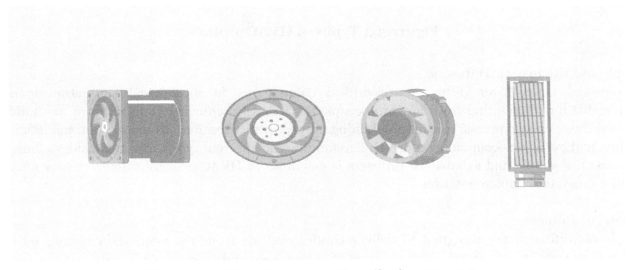

Figure 3.2 Heat Recovery Ventilation Duct Fan

Design Considerations:
Designing HRV and ERV systems involves careful selection of the appropriate heat exchanger type, sizing, and efficiency. The heat exchanger's effectiveness in transferring thermal energy and moisture between the two air streams is critical to maximizing energy recovery and reducing the workload on heating or cooling systems. Additionally, the design must account for air distribution, pressure differentials, and control mechanisms to ensure optimal energy recovery and ventilation performance.

Pros and Cons:

HRV and ERV systems offer significant energy savings by pre-conditioning the incoming fresh air, reducing the heating or cooling load required to achieve comfortable indoor conditions. By recovering heat and moisture, these systems enhance indoor comfort and reduce energy consumption. However, the installation and maintenance of HRV and ERV systems may require a higher initial investment, and their efficiency depends on climate conditions and usage patterns.

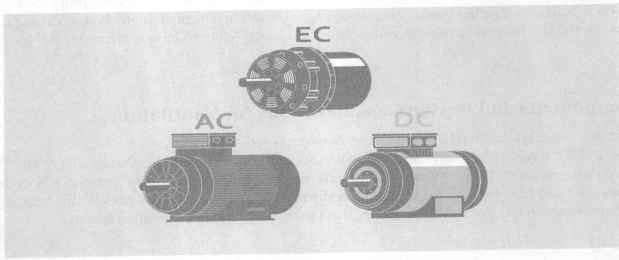

Figure 3.3 Types of HVAC Motors

Supply and Exhaust Air Diffusers:
Supply and exhaust air diffusers are critical components in mechanical ventilation systems, responsible for distributing fresh air into occupied spaces and removing stale air from the building. These diffusers play a pivotal role in maintaining proper air distribution, promoting optimal indoor air quality, and ensuring occupant comfort. Understanding the different types, design considerations, and placement of supply and exhaust air diffusers is essential for HVAC professionals to master effective ventilation system implementation.

Supply Air Diffusers:
Supply air diffusers are designed to deliver conditioned air from the ventilation system into the occupied spaces. They are strategically located to ensure even and efficient air distribution throughout the room. Key design considerations for supply air diffusers include:

Airflow Pattern: Supply air diffusers are available in various airflow patterns, including radial, linear, and perforated designs. The choice of diffuser type depends on the room's layout, air distribution requirements, and occupant comfort preferences.

Air Throw: The distance that supply air can travel from the diffuser, known as air throw, should match the room's dimensions and ventilation needs. Proper air throw ensures that conditioned air reaches the occupied zone and prevents stagnation or dead zones.

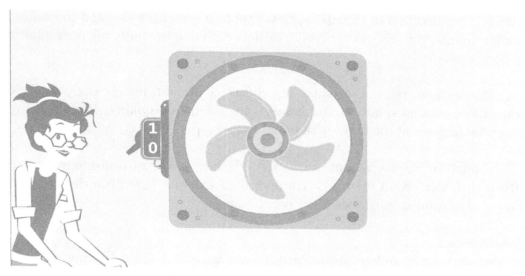

Figure 3.4 Air Diffusers Fan

Air Volume Control: Many supply air diffusers offer adjustable louvers or dampers, allowing occupants to regulate the air volume and direction. Individual comfort preferences can be accommodated by providing control over the airflow in specific areas.

Noise Level: The design of supply air diffusers should minimize noise generation, particularly in quiet spaces such as offices, bedrooms, or libraries. Low-noise diffusers contribute to improved occupant comfort and productivity.

Exhaust Air Diffusers:
Exhaust air diffusers serve the critical function of removing stale air, odors, and pollutants from the building. They are strategically placed in areas where contaminants are generated to facilitate effective air extraction. Key design considerations for exhaust air diffusers include:

Figure 3.5 Airflow Direction

Airflow Direction: The direction of exhaust airflow should be carefully planned to ensure the effective removal of contaminants from the room. Proper airflow direction prevents the recirculation of stale air back into the occupied zone.

Airflow Rate: The airflow rate of exhaust air diffusers should match the room's contaminant generation rate to ensure adequate air exchange and indoor air quality. Proper sizing of exhaust diffusers is essential to prevent the buildup of pollutants.

Vent Design: Exhaust air diffusers come in various designs, such as wall-mounted grilles, ceiling-mounted diffusers, or dedicated ductwork connected to exhaust fans. The design should promote efficient airflow and minimize resistance to air movement.

Placement Considerations:
Proper placement of supply and exhaust air diffusers is crucial for achieving optimal ventilation performance. Some important considerations include:

Airflow Distribution: Supply air diffusers should be placed strategically to promote uniform airflow distribution throughout the room, avoiding drafts or dead spots. Proper airflow distribution contributes to consistent indoor comfort.

Contaminant Removal: Exhaust air diffusers should be located in proximity to pollutant sources, such as cooking areas, bathrooms, or industrial spaces. Placing exhaust diffusers close to contaminants ensures their efficient removal from the room.

Pressure Balancing: Ensuring a balanced airflow between supply and exhaust systems prevents the building from becoming negatively pressurized, which can lead to air infiltration from undesirable locations. Proper pressure balancing is crucial for maintaining indoor air quality and energy efficiency.

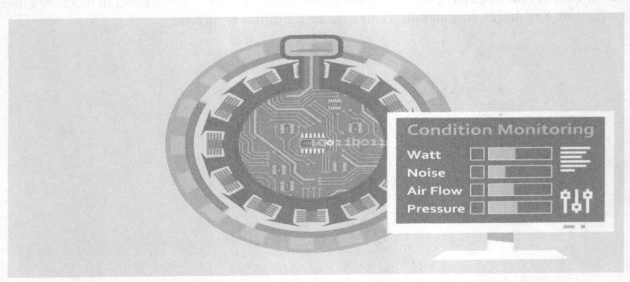

Figure 3.6 Local Codes and Regulations Condition Monitoring

Local Codes and Regulations: Adherence to building codes and regulations is essential when determining the placement of supply and exhaust air diffusers. Codes may specify minimum distance requirements from walls, ceilings, or other obstructions to ensure optimal ventilation.

Supply and exhaust air diffusers are integral components of mechanical ventilation systems, enabling effective air distribution, contaminant removal, and occupant comfort. By considering factors such as airflow patterns, air throw, noise levels, airflow direction, and proper placement, HVAC professionals can ensure efficient ventilation, enhance indoor air quality, and create a healthy and comfortable indoor environment. These components, when thoughtfully selected and properly integrated within the ventilation system, contribute to overall energy efficiency and occupant well-being.

Ventilation System Balancing and Testing

Ventilation System Balancing and Testing:
Balancing a ventilation system is a pivotal process that guarantees optimum performance, uniform airflow distribution, and occupant comfort. It involves meticulous adjustments to individual components to achieve harmonized and balanced ventilation throughout the building. Properly balanced ventilation systems ensure consistent indoor air quality, prevent air pressure discrepancies, and maximize HVAC system energy efficiency. In this context, we will delve into the intricacies of the balancing process and the key considerations entailed in balancing a ventilation system.

Significance of Balancing:
Balancing a ventilation system bears immense importance for the following reasons:

Airflow Distribution: Balancing ensures the even distribution of air throughout the building, affording consistent ventilation across all occupied spaces. It eradicates areas with either excessive airflow or inadequate air supply, thereby fostering a comfortable and healthy indoor environment.

Occupant Comfort: Balanced airflow sustains uniform room temperatures and averts drafts, establishing a comfortable living or working environment for building occupants.

Energy Efficiency: Through balancing, airflow rates can be optimized to match the unique needs of each space. Consequently, unnecessary energy consumption is circumvented, resulting in reduced operational costs.

Equipment Performance: Proper airflow balancing ensures that ventilation equipment, such as fans and dampers, operate within their designated design parameters, enhancing their efficiency and lifespan.

The Balancing Process:
The balancing process typically involves the following steps:

System Assessment: An evaluation of the entire ventilation system, including components, ductwork, fans, and dampers, identifies any issues necessitating adjustments during the balancing process.

Airflow Measurements: Specialized instruments like anemometers, flow hoods, or flow sensors are used to measure airflow rates at various points within the system. These measurements furnish quantitative data regarding actual airflow rates in different areas.

Adjustments and Balancing: Based on the airflow measurements, adjustments are made to individual components, such as dampers, fan speeds, or ductwork configurations. The objective is to balance the airflow to meet the specific ventilation requirements of each space while maintaining an overall airflow balance.

Verification and Testing: After adjustments are completed, airflow measurements are taken again to verify that the desired airflow rates have been achieved. This step ensures that the ventilation system is appropriately balanced and performing as intended.

Considerations for Balancing:
Balancing a ventilation system requires careful consideration of various factors:

Design Specifications: The balancing process should align with the design specifications and recommendations provided by the system manufacturer or HVAC engineer to ensure the system operates within its intended design parameters.

Occupancy and Use: Airflow requirements may vary based on the occupancy and use of different spaces within the building. Spaces with higher occupancy or specific ventilation needs may require higher airflow rates compared to less frequently occupied areas.

Pressure Balancing: Pressure differentials between rooms should be considered during the balancing process to prevent issues like air leakage, infiltration, or uncomfortable drafts. Proper pressure balancing helps maintain a consistent indoor environment and prevents air transfer between areas with different pressure levels.

Regular Maintenance: Balancing is an ongoing task. Periodic review and adjustment of the ventilation system are essential to account for changes in occupancy, building layout modifications, or aging of system components. Regular maintenance ensures that the system remains properly balanced over time.

Ventilation System Testing and Airflow Measurement:

Accurate airflow measurement and thorough testing are integral aspects of assessing the performance of a ventilation system. Precise measurements help ensure the system operates at optimal levels, delivers the required airflow rates, and maintains a comfortable indoor environment. Through airflow measurement and testing, HVAC professionals can identify and rectify any deficiencies or imbalances, leading to improved system efficiency and occupant satisfaction. Let's explore the importance of airflow measurement and the various methods used in testing ventilation systems.

Importance of Airflow Measurement:

Accurate airflow measurement serves several crucial purposes within a ventilation system:

Balancing: Airflow measurement determines the actual airflow rates in different parts of the system, facilitating proper balancing and adjustments to achieve uniform air distribution throughout the building.

Performance Evaluation: By comparing measured airflow rates with the design specifications, HVAC professionals can assess the system's performance and identify any deviations or deficiencies that may impact efficiency, air quality, or occupant comfort.

Troubleshooting: Airflow measurement aids in troubleshooting issues within the ventilation system. It enables the identification of airflow restrictions, duct leaks, improper damper operation, or fan inefficiencies, allowing for timely corrective actions.

Energy Efficiency: Accurate airflow measurement optimizes the operation of fans, dampers, and other components, resulting in improved energy efficiency and reduced operational costs.

Methods of Airflow Measurement:

Various methods can be used to measure airflow within a ventilation system. Some commonly employed techniques include:

Anemometers: Anemometers measure airflow velocity using sensors like vane, hot-wire, or thermal anemometers. These handheld devices are placed at specific locations within the ductwork or near supply and exhaust grilles to measure airflow speed. By combining velocity measurements with cross-sectional area calculations, airflow rates can be determined.

Flow Hoods: Flow hoods are specialized tools used to measure airflow rates at supply and exhaust grilles. These hoods are placed over the grille, creating a capture area where airflow is directed. By measuring the pressure differential across the hood and accounting for the capture area, the airflow rate can be determined.

Pitot Tubes: Pitot tubes measure airflow velocity within ducts. They consist of a tube with a small opening (static pressure port) and an extended opening (total pressure port) facing the airflow. By comparing the static and total pressures, the velocity pressure and, subsequently, the airflow rate can be calculated.

Flow Sensors: Flow sensors, such as thermal dispersion or differential pressure-based sensors, can be installed within ducts or at specific locations to provide continuous airflow measurements. These sensors use various principles to estimate airflow rates based on changes in temperature, pressure, or flow characteristics.

Testing Procedures:

In addition to airflow measurement, testing procedures are crucial to assess the overall performance of a ventilation system. Some common testing procedures include:

Air Leakage Testing: This test evaluates the integrity of the ductwork by measuring air leakage rates. It helps identify potential leaks and areas where air may escape or infiltrate the system, affecting overall efficiency and airflow distribution.

Pressure Differential Testing: Pressure differential testing is performed to ensure proper pressure balancing within the building. By measuring pressure differentials between rooms and spaces, HVAC professionals can identify areas with excessive or inadequate pressure, allowing for necessary adjustments.

Air Change Rate Testing: Air change rate testing involves measuring the rate at which the air within a specific space is replaced with fresh outdoor air. This test helps determine if the ventilation system is providing the desired air exchange rate to maintain indoor air quality and occupant comfort.

Noise Testing: Noise levels generated by ventilation components, such as fans and ductwork, can impact occupant comfort. Noise testing helps evaluate the acoustic performance of the system, ensuring that noise levels are within acceptable limits.

Calibration and Accuracy:

To ensure accurate airflow measurement and testing, it is essential to regularly calibrate the measurement devices and instruments used. Calibration helps maintain the accuracy and reliability of the equipment, ensuring that the measurements obtained are precise and consistent.

Adherence to accepted industry standards and guidelines for airflow measurement and testing, such as those established by groups like ASHRAE (American Society of Heating, Refrigerating, and Air-Conditioning Engineers), further ensures the correct and consistent execution of procedures.

Conclusion:

Accurate airflow measurement and thorough testing are critical for maintaining the performance, efficiency, and comfort of a ventilation system. Employing appropriate measurement techniques, conducting comprehensive testing procedures, and adhering to calibration standards are vital steps in optimizing system operation, effectively troubleshooting issues, and providing building occupants with a healthy and comfortable indoor environment. Through meticulous airflow measurement and testing, HVAC professionals can ensure the successful implementation and maintenance of efficient ventilation systems.

Indoor Air Quality and Filtration Techniques

Indoor Air Pollutants

Due to the fact that people spend a lot of time indoors, particularly in residential and commercial buildings, indoor air quality (IAQ) is a major concern. Understanding and addressing the origins and consequences of indoor air pollution is essential because they can have a negative influence on human health and comfort. Indoor settings may contain a variety of contaminants that come from both internal and external sources. Let's look at some typical indoor air contaminants and their possible negative impacts on health.

Volatile Organic Compounds (VOCs):
Organic substances known as VOCs have the ability to evaporate at ambient temperature and release potentially dangerous gases into the atmosphere. They are frequently discovered in a variety of home goods, such as paints, cleaners, adhesives, and furniture. Long-term health problems, headaches, dizziness, and irritated eyes, noses, and throats can all result from exposure to VOCs. The management of VOC sources should include adequate ventilation, the use of low-emitting products, and routine monitoring.

Particulate Matter:
Tiny solid or liquid particles suspended in the air are referred to as particulate matter. Dust, pollen, pet dander, mold spores, and combustion byproducts from cooking, smoking, or burning fuels are examples of sources of particulate matter. These airborne particles have the potential to irritate already-existing respiratory disorders like asthma and cause allergies as well as other respiratory symptoms. Particulate matter can be lessened inside with effective filtration and routine cleaning.

Carbon Monoxide (CO):
A colorless, odorless gas called carbon monoxide is created when fossil fuels like gas, oil, and wood burn partially. Combustion appliances like stoves, fireplaces, and furnaces that are broken or poorly maintained can emit CO into enclosed rooms. High levels of CO can be inhaled and cause symptoms such as nausea, headaches, and carbon monoxide poisoning, which can be fatal. For the purpose of reducing CO buildup, proper ventilation and routine combustion appliance inspection are essential.

Radon:
A naturally occurring radioactive gas called radon can enter buildings through flaws in the foundation or in the materials used to build them. Long-term exposure to high radon levels, especially in places with high radon concentrations, is a significant risk factor for lung cancer. To lower radon levels and ensure a safe indoor environment, mitigation measures must be put in place, including crack sealing and the installation of radon mitigation devices.

Biological Contaminants:
Numerous microorganisms, including bacteria, viruses, mold, and dust mites, are examples of biological pollutants. These contaminants can flourish in moist conditions, in regions with high humidity levels, and in ventilation systems that are not properly maintained. Allergies, respiratory infections, and other health problems can be brought on by exposure to biological pollutants. In order to stop the accumulation and spread of biological contaminants, it is essential to maintain HVAC systems on a regular basis and to properly ventilate the space and control the humidity.

Formaldehyde:

Formaldehyde is a colorless gas used in the production of building materials, furniture, and household products. It can be released into the air from sources like pressed wood products, carpets, and upholstery. Prolonged exposure to formaldehyde can irritate the respiratory system, leading to respiratory symptoms and, in some cases, may increase the risk of certain cancers. Adequate ventilation and selecting low-emitting products can help reduce formaldehyde levels indoors.

Filtration Systems and Filters
Filtration systems play a crucial role in maintaining good indoor air quality (IAQ) by removing airborne contaminants and particulate matter from the air. These systems are designed to capture and trap pollutants, allergens, and other harmful particles, preventing them from circulating and being inhaled by building occupants. Let's explore the importance of filtration systems and the different types of filters commonly used.

Importance of Filtration Systems
Filtration systems are essential for several reasons:

Particle Removal: Filtration systems effectively remove airborne particles such as dust, pollen, pet dander, mold spores, and other allergens from the indoor air. This helps reduce the risk of respiratory issues, allergies, and asthma symptoms among occupants.

Improved Indoor Air Quality: By removing pollutants, filtration systems contribute to maintaining a cleaner and healthier indoor environment, free from harmful contaminants. This is particularly important for individuals with sensitivities or respiratory conditions.

Protection of HVAC Equipment: Filtration systems help prevent the buildup of dust and debris on HVAC components such as coils, fans, and heat exchangers. This reduces the risk of equipment malfunction, improves system efficiency, and extends the lifespan of the HVAC system.

Types of Filters
Filtration systems employ various types of filters to capture and remove particles from the air. The choice of filter depends on the specific requirements of the building and the desired level of filtration. Here are some common types of filters:

Mechanical Filters: Mechanical filters, also known as particulate filters, are designed to physically trap particles as air passes through the filter media. These filters use a dense material, such as fiberglass, pleated fabric, or synthetic fibers, to capture particles of various sizes. Mechanical filters are often rated based on their efficiency in removing particles of specific sizes, indicated by the Minimum Efficiency Reporting Value (MERV) rating. Higher MERV ratings indicate higher filtration efficiency.

High-Efficiency Particulate Air (HEPA) Filters: HEPA filters are a type of mechanical filter that has a 99.97% efficiency rate and can catch particles as small as 0.3 microns. Dust, pollen, mold spores, as well as some germs and viruses, are among the small particles that HEPA filters are very good at eliminating. In settings where air quality is important, such hospitals, labs, and cleanrooms, they are frequently used.

Filters with activated carbon: Filters with activated carbon absorb specific gases, smells, and chemical vapors using a porous carbon substance. These filters work well to eliminate noxious aromas, volatile organic compounds (VOCs), and pollutants from the air. For thorough air purification, activated carbon filters are frequently coupled with other filter types.

Electrostatic Filters: Electrostatic filters use an electric charge to attract and capture particles as air passes through the filter media. These filters can be washable or disposable and are effective in removing larger particles, including dust and pet dander. Electrostatic filters are often reusable and can be cleaned regularly to maintain their efficiency.

UV-C filters are used to kill or deactivate microorganisms like bacteria, viruses, and mold spores by exposing them to ultraviolet (UV) radiation. These filters usually come with the HVAC system and cooperate with other filters to offer improved germicidal defense. Particularly helpful are UV-C filters in locations where biological pollutants are an issue.

Maintenance and Replacement
Filtration systems must be properly maintained and its filters must be changed on a regular basis. Filters lose efficiency and limit airflow as they accumulate trapped particles over time. It's crucial to go by the manufacturer's instructions and suggestions for filter replacement cycles. Filters should be regularly inspected, cleaned, and replaced to maintain airflow and sustain improvements in IAQ.

Additional Indoor Air Quality Measures
In addition to filtration systems, there are several other measures that can be implemented to further enhance indoor air quality (IAQ). These measures target different aspects of IAQ management and work in conjunction with filtration systems to create a healthier and more comfortable indoor environment. Let's explore some additional IAQ measures that can be adopted.

Source Control:
Source control focuses on minimizing or eliminating the sources of indoor air pollutants. This involves identifying and addressing potential pollutant sources such as chemicals, off-gassing materials, and cleaning agents. By selecting low-emitting or environmentally friendly products, properly storing chemicals, and controlling pollutant sources, the introduction of harmful substances into the indoor air can be reduced.

Proper Ventilation:
Adequate ventilation is crucial for maintaining good IAQ. It involves the exchange of stale indoor air with fresh outdoor air. Proper ventilation helps dilute and remove indoor pollutants, replenishes oxygen levels, and controls excess humidity. There are different ventilation strategies, including natural ventilation, mechanical ventilation, and a combination of both. The ventilation system should be designed and maintained to meet recommended airflow rates and provide sufficient air exchange based on building occupancy and usage.
Humidity Control:
Excessive humidity levels can lead to mold growth, increased dust mite populations, and the proliferation of other biological contaminants. On the other hand, low humidity can cause discomfort and respiratory issues. Maintaining optimal humidity levels between 30% and 50% can help prevent

these problems. Humidity control measures include the use of dehumidifiers, humidifiers, and proper ventilation strategies to manage moisture levels effectively.

Regular Cleaning and Maintenance:
Regular cleaning and maintenance practices are essential for keeping the indoor environment clean and reducing the accumulation of dust, allergens, and pollutants. This includes routine cleaning of floors, surfaces, carpets, and furniture. HVAC system maintenance, such as regular inspection, cleaning of ductwork, and changing or cleaning filters, is also crucial. Proper maintenance ensures the efficient operation of the system and reduces the risk of contamination and pollutant recirculation.

Indoor Plants:
Indoor plants can serve as natural air purifiers by absorbing some pollutants and releasing oxygen. Certain plant species, such as peace lilies, spider plants, and snake plants, have been found to be effective in improving IAQ. Incorporating indoor plants in the living or working spaces can provide a visual appeal while contributing to a healthier indoor environment.

IAQ Monitoring:
Implementing IAQ monitoring systems allows for real-time monitoring and assessment of indoor air quality parameters. These systems can measure factors such as temperature, humidity, carbon dioxide (CO_2) levels, and volatile organic compounds (VOCs). By continuously monitoring IAQ, potential issues can be detected early, and appropriate measures can be taken to maintain optimal indoor conditions.

Education and Awareness:
Educating building occupants about IAQ, its importance, and the role they can play in maintaining a healthy indoor environment is crucial. This includes promoting good habits such as proper waste disposal, regular ventilation practices, and reporting any concerns related to IAQ. Raising awareness helps foster a collective effort in maintaining and improving IAQ within the building.

Book 4

Air Conditioning Fundamentals

Principles of Refrigeration and Air Conditioning

Introduction to refrigeration and air conditioning

Refrigeration and air conditioning are integral to our daily lives, providing comfort and convenience in our homes, workplaces, and various industries. These systems play a vital role in maintaining suitable temperature and humidity levels, creating a comfortable environment, preserving perishable goods, and facilitating numerous industrial processes. To understand the principles behind refrigeration and air conditioning, it is essential to delve into their fundamental concepts and functions.

Removing heat from a place or thing results in refrigeration, which lowers temperatures. It entails the mechanical, thermal, or chemical transfer of heat from a low-temperature region to a high-temperature one. By eliminating heat energy, refrigeration's fundamental objective is to generate and maintain a cold environment. This procedure is essential for protecting perishable goods including food, drinks, pharmaceuticals, and other goods from spoiling and extending their shelf lives.

On the other hand, air conditioning focuses on preserving acceptable indoor air quality and thermal comfort. It entails regulating the temperature, humidity, airflow, and ventilation to provide occupants with a comfortable and healthy environment. Air conditioning systems ensure maximum comfort in a variety of situations, including residential, commercial, and industrial environments, by providing relief from extreme heat, high humidity, or frigid temperatures.

The fundamentals of heat transmission serve as the basis for refrigeration and air conditioning. Conduction, convection, and radiation are the three basic ways that heat can be moved from one location to another. Conduction is the direct passage of heat between two materials or objects. Heat is transferred via convection when a fluid, such as air or water, is moving. Emission and absorption of electromagnetic waves, which are capable of transferring heat energy, constitute radiation.

To achieve refrigeration and air conditioning, a refrigerant plays a critical role. Refrigerants are substances with specific properties that allow them to absorb and release heat efficiently. They undergo phase changes from a low-pressure gas to a high-pressure liquid and vice versa, enabling the transfer of heat in the process. Commonly used refrigerants include hydrofluorocarbons (HFCs), hydrochlorofluorocarbons (HCFCs), and natural refrigerants like ammonia and carbon dioxide.

In recent years, environmental considerations have become increasingly important in refrigeration and air conditioning systems. Certain refrigerants, such as chlorofluorocarbons (CFCs) and hydrochlorofluorocarbons (HCFCs), have been identified as contributors to ozone depletion and climate change. As a result, global regulations and agreements have been implemented to phase out the use of such substances, promoting the adoption of more environmentally friendly alternatives with lower global warming potential (GWP).

Understanding the Refrigeration Cycle

Any refrigeration or air conditioning system's primary component is the refrigeration cycle. It is a continuous process that enables heat to be moved from a low-temperature region to a high-temperature region, effectively cooling the first area. Understanding the compressor, condenser, expansion valve, and evaporator—the cycle's four main parts—is crucial for understanding refrigeration.

Compressor: The compressor raises the pressure and temperature of the refrigerant gas by compressing the gas. As it circulates the refrigerant and starts the complete refrigeration cycle, it serves as the system's beating heart. The low-pressure refrigerant vapor is compressed by the compressor, which raises its temperature dramatically and turns it into a high-pressure gas.

Condenser: The high-pressure refrigerant gas enters the condenser after exiting the compressor. The refrigerant can release heat to the environment through the condenser, which causes it to condense and change into a high-pressure liquid. This process takes place as air or water passes through the condenser coils and receives heat from the refrigerant. As a result, the refrigerant starts to cool down and lose heat energy.

Expansion Valve: The refrigerant travels through the expansion valve after condensing into a high-pressure liquid. The refrigerant's pressure and temperature are reduced via the expansion valve, which has a tiny, confined aperture. A abrupt reduction in pressure occurs as the refrigerant travels through the expansion valve, causing it to expand quickly. The temperature drops noticeably as a result of the expansion, turning the refrigerant into a low-pressure, low-temperature mixture of liquid and vapor.

Evaporator: After passing through the evaporator, the low-pressure refrigerant mixture absorbs heat from the air or water in the air conditioning system. The refrigerant evaporates and returns to becoming a low-pressure vapor when it absorbs heat. The evaporator's air or water cools down as a result of this heat absorption process, producing the required cooling effect. The refrigeration cycle is then restarted by drawing the low-pressure vapor back into the compressor.

Understanding the refrigeration cycle is crucial for diagnosing and troubleshooting issues in refrigeration and air conditioning systems. By comprehending how the different components work together, technicians can identify problems such as low cooling capacity, refrigerant leaks, or inefficient operation, and take appropriate corrective measures.

Refrigerants and Their Properties
Refrigerants are central to the operation of refrigeration and air conditioning systems. These substances undergo phase changes and transfer heat energy, allowing for the cooling effect within the system. Over the years, various types of refrigerants have been used, each with its own set of properties and environmental considerations.

Chlorofluorocarbons (CFCs): CFCs were once widely used as refrigerants due to their excellent thermodynamic properties and non-flammability. However, it was discovered that CFCs contribute to ozone depletion when released into the atmosphere. As a result, their production and use have been phased out under international agreements such as the Montreal Protocol.

Hydrochlorofluorocarbons (HCFCs): HCFCs were introduced as transitional substitutes for CFCs. While they have lower ozone depletion potential compared to CFCs, they still contribute to ozone depletion and are being phased out globally. HCFCs, such as R-22, have been widely used in older air conditioning systems but are being replaced by more environmentally friendly alternatives.

Hydrofluorocarbons (HFCs): HFCs emerged as the primary replacement for CFCs and HCFCs due to their negligible ozone depletion potential. They do not contain chlorine, which makes them ozone-friendly. However, HFCs have high global warming potential (GWP), meaning they have the potential to contribute to climate change. Common HFC refrigerants include R-134a, R-410A, and R-404A.

Natural Refrigerants: In response to environmental concerns, natural refrigerants have gained popularity as sustainable alternatives. These include ammonia (R-717), carbon dioxide (R-744), and hydrocarbons like propane (R-290) and butane (R-600a). Natural refrigerants have low or zero GWP and ozone depletion potential, making them environmentally friendly options. However, they require careful handling due to their flammability or toxicity properties.

The choice of a refrigerant is influenced by a number of elements, including as the needs of the system, energy efficiency, environmental impact, safety considerations, and local laws. The unique characteristics of each refrigerant, such as its pressure-temperature characteristics, thermodynamic performance, flammability, and toxicity, must be taken into account. New refrigerants are continually being developed as a result of technological breakthroughs, offering increased efficiency and less environmental effect.

Environmental Considerations and Regulations

Environmental factors have grown in significance in the refrigeration and air conditioning industries during the last few decades. Refrigerants have a negative impact on the ozone layer and climate change, which has prompted the creation of standards and laws aimed at lessening the environmental impact of these systems. The responsible design, installation, and operation of refrigeration and air conditioning systems depends on awareness of these environmental factors and adherence to pertinent legislation.

Ozone Depletion Potential (ODP): When a material is discharged into the atmosphere, it has the potential to thin out the ozone layer. The ozone layer is being destroyed by hydrochlorofluorocarbons (HCFCs) and chlorofluorocarbons (CFCs), which have been discovered to have significant ODP. As a result, under international accords like the Montreal Protocol, their production and consumption have been gradually reduced. As a result of the phase-out of ozone-depleting compounds, alternative refrigerants with reduced or zero ODP have become more common.

The term "global warming potential" (GWP) refers to a substance's capacity to trap heat in the atmosphere and hence influence climate change. Hydrofluorocarbons (HFCs), a class of high-GWP refrigerants, have drawn attention because of their large contribution to global warming. Despite not reducing the ozone layer, their high GWP has prompted searches for substitute refrigerants with lower GWP. The Kigali Amendment to the Montreal Protocol seeks to accelerate the adoption of low-GWP substitutes while gradually reducing the production and use of high-GWP HFCs.

The Montreal Protocol and the Kigali Amendment are two international environmental treaties that were formed in 1987 to save the ozone layer. The manufacture and consumption of ozone-depleting compounds, such as CFCs and HCFCs, have to be phased out. The Montreal Protocol's reach has been expanded by the Kigali Amendment, which was ratified in 2016, to cover the phase-out of HFCs. The amendment establishes precise goals and deadlines for lowering HFC production and usage in participating nations, promoting the switch to more ecologically friendly substitutes.

Refrigerant Management: Proper refrigerant management is essential to minimize environmental impact. This includes strategies such as reducing refrigerant leakage, implementing effective recovery and recycling programs, and ensuring proper disposal of refrigerants at the end of their lifecycle. Technicians and system owners should be aware of regulations governing refrigerant handling, storage, and disposal to prevent environmental contamination and promote sustainable practices.

Energy Efficiency: Energy efficiency is a crucial aspect of environmental considerations in refrigeration and air conditioning. Highly efficient systems reduce energy consumption, resulting in lower greenhouse gas emissions. Energy efficiency measures include proper system sizing, regular maintenance, insulation improvements, and the use of advanced technologies such as variable speed drives and energy recovery systems. Energy efficiency regulations and standards, such as SEER (Seasonal Energy Efficiency Ratio) and EER (Energy Efficiency Ratio), provide guidelines for manufacturers and promote the use of efficient equipment.

Eco-Design and Labels: Many countries have implemented eco-design requirements for energy-consuming products, including refrigeration and air conditioning systems. These regulations set minimum energy efficiency standards and may include labeling schemes to provide consumers with information about the energy performance of appliances. Compliance with eco-design regulations ensures that products meet specific environmental and energy efficiency criteria, contributing to sustainable practices.

By considering environmental factors and complying with regulations, the refrigeration and air conditioning industry can reduce its impact on the ozone layer and climate change. Adhering to responsible practices, adopting low-GWP refrigerants, implementing energy-efficient technologies, and promoting proper refrigerant management contribute to a more sustainable and environmentally friendly approach to refrigeration and air conditioning.

Types of Air Conditioning Systems

Window Air Conditioners:

Window air conditioners are affordable and popular choices for cooling individual rooms or small spaces. These units are installed in windows or wall holes for efficient cooling. They consist of essential components like an evaporator coil, compressor, condenser, and expansion valve. Refrigerant gas circulates, changing phases to absorb heat from the ambient air and release it outside. Installation involves securing the unit with brackets, screws, or a window installation kit to ensure proper sealing for maximum cooling efficiency.

Split Air Conditioning Systems:

Split air conditioning systems are versatile options for cooling larger areas or multiple rooms. They comprise two main units: an indoor unit with an evaporator coil and fan, and an outdoor unit with a compressor and condenser coil. The two units are connected by refrigerant lines and electrical wiring. Split systems offer flexibility in installation, with the indoor unit mounted on walls, ceilings, or floors. They provide quiet operation, energy efficiency, and the ability to control temperature settings in different zones.

Central Air Conditioning Systems:

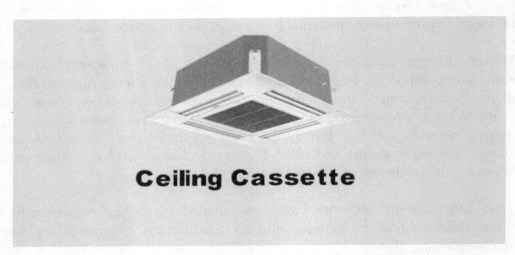

Figure 4.1 Central Air Conditioning Systems

Central air conditioning systems efficiently cool large spaces or entire buildings. They consist of a condensing unit with a compressor, condenser coil, and fan located outside, and an indoor unit with an evaporator coil and blower. Ductwork distributes cooled air throughout the building, and zoning capabilities allow personalized temperature control in different areas. Central systems boast high energy efficiency due to advanced technologies like variable-speed compressors and programmable thermostats.

Heat Pumps:

Heat pumps provide both cooling and heating capabilities. They exchange heat energy between indoors and outdoors, allowing them to cool in summer and heat in winter. Heat pumps have an interior unit with an evaporator coil and blower, and an outdoor unit with a compressor and condenser coil. They offer energy-efficient operation and significant cost savings compared to conventional systems.

Ductless Mini-Split Systems:

Ductless mini-split systems, also called ductless air conditioners or ductless heat pumps, are ideal for buildings without ductwork. They consist of an outdoor unit with a compressor and condenser coil, and one or more indoor units with evaporator coils and fans. Each indoor unit cools or heats a specific zone, providing individualized temperature control. Ductless mini-split systems are energy-efficient, easy to install, and allow for quiet operation.

Ducted Air Conditioning Systems:

Ducted air conditioning systems are centralized cooling solutions that utilize a network of ducts to distribute conditioned air throughout the building. These systems are commonly used in larger residential and commercial buildings, providing consistent cooling in multiple rooms or zones. Ducted systems consist of essential components like the condensing unit, evaporator coil, blower fan, and a series of ducts.

Operation and Components:

The ducted air conditioning process starts with the condensing unit located outside the building. The compressor and condenser coil circulate refrigerant, changing its phase from a low-pressure vapor to a high-pressure liquid. The refrigerant flows through the evaporator coil inside the air handler, where it absorbs heat from the indoor air, cooling it down. The blower fan then circulates the cooled air through the ducts and distributes it to various rooms or areas.

Ductwork and Air Distribution:

Ducted air conditioning relies on a system of ducts to distribute cooled air efficiently. Properly designed and sized ductwork ensures optimal airflow and temperature distribution, maintaining consistent comfort levels throughout the building. The ducts are strategically placed in the walls, ceilings, or floors, and they may have dampers to control airflow to different areas.

Zoning and Temperature Control:

Ducted air conditioning systems often feature zoning capabilities, allowing users to create customized temperature zones within the building. Zoning is achieved through motorized dampers in the ductwork, which can open or close to regulate airflow to specific zones. Each zone has its own thermostat, enabling individual temperature control, and optimizing energy efficiency by cooling or heating only the occupied areas.

Energy Efficiency and Air Leakage:

Efficient duct design and regular maintenance are crucial for energy efficiency in ducted air conditioning systems. Properly insulated and sealed ducts minimize air leakage, preventing cooled air from escaping and reducing energy waste. Periodic duct inspection and cleaning ensure optimal airflow and indoor air quality, enhancing system performance and reducing energy consumption.

Maintenance and Servicing:

Regular maintenance is essential for the optimal functioning and longevity of ducted air conditioning systems. Maintenance tasks include inspecting and cleaning the evaporator and condenser coils, checking refrigerant levels, cleaning or replacing air filters, and verifying electrical connections. Additionally, ducts should be inspected for leaks and properly sealed to prevent energy losses.

Conclusion:

Understanding the technical aspects of various air conditioning systems is vital for HVAC professionals to make informed decisions in selecting, installing, and maintaining these systems for different applications. Each type of system offers unique features and benefits, catering to specific cooling requirements and preferences. By considering factors like energy efficiency, installation flexibility, and maintenance needs, HVAC experts can design and implement optimal cooling solutions for residential, commercial, and industrial settings, ensuring comfort and satisfaction for occupants while maximizing energy savings.

Components of Air Conditioning Systems

Expansion Valves and Metering Devices:
Expansion valves and metering devices are crucial components in air conditioning systems that regulate the flow of refrigerant and control the cooling process. Their primary functions involve carefully managing the refrigerant flow into the evaporator coils, enabling efficient heat absorption, and maintaining optimal system performance. Let's delve into the functions and features of expansion valves and metering devices in more detail.

Expansion Valves:
Expansion valves are critical for precisely controlling the refrigerant flow into the evaporator coils. They play a key role in allowing the refrigerant to undergo a controlled pressure drop and temperature reduction as it enters the evaporator. This enables efficient heat absorption from the indoor air and ensures the proper cooling process.

Operating based on pressure regulation principles, expansion valves continuously monitor the refrigerant's pressure and temperature as it exits the evaporator coils. They adjust the flow rate accordingly to ensure the evaporator operates at the optimal pressure and temperature for effective heat absorption.

There are various types of expansion valves used in air conditioning systems, including:

Thermostatic Expansion Valves (TXVs): TXVs are commonly employed in residential and commercial air conditioning systems. These valves regulate refrigerant flow based on the superheat of the refrigerant gas leaving the evaporator. Superheat is the difference between the actual refrigerant temperature and its saturation temperature at a specific pressure.

Electronic Expansion Valves (EEVs): Utilizing electronic controls and sensors, EEVs offer precise control over refrigerant flow. They are commonly found in advanced or high-efficiency air conditioning systems, providing accurate regulation.

Selecting the appropriate expansion valve and ensuring proper sizing are crucial to achieving optimal system performance. Regular maintenance and inspection of expansion valves are essential to keep them clean, free from debris, and operating correctly.

Metering Devices:
Metering devices, also known as refrigerant flow control devices, are responsible for regulating the refrigerant flow rate between the condenser and evaporator coils. These devices create a pressure difference that controls the refrigerant's entry into the evaporator, maintaining the desired balance between its liquid and vapor phases.

The main types of metering devices used in air conditioning systems include:

Fixed Orifice: Fixed orifice metering devices, such as capillary tubes or fixed-size orifices, have a fixed opening size that restricts the flow of refrigerant. They are simple in design and commonly used in smaller air conditioning units or systems with relatively consistent cooling demands.

Thermostatic Expansion Valve (TXV): As mentioned earlier, TXVs not only act as expansion valves but also serve as metering devices. They regulate refrigerant flow based on the superheat of the refrigerant gas leaving the evaporator.

Automatic Metering Devices: Automatic metering devices, such as electronic expansion valves or electronic flow control devices, use electronic controls to modulate the refrigerant flow based on system demands. These devices offer precise control and adaptability to varying cooling requirements.

Heat Exchangers and Fans:

Heat exchangers and fans are vital components in air conditioning systems that facilitate the transfer of heat and ensure proper airflow within the system. These components work together to optimize the cooling process and maintain the desired indoor climate. Let's explore the functions and features of heat exchangers and fans in more detail.

Heat Exchangers:

Heat exchangers play a critical role in air conditioning systems by facilitating the transfer of thermal energy between the refrigerant and the surrounding air. They exist in both the evaporator and condenser coils, where heat exchange occurs during the cooling and heating processes.

Evaporator Coil: In the evaporator coil, heat exchangers absorb heat from the indoor air, causing the refrigerant to evaporate and change from a liquid to a low-pressure vapor. This heat absorption results in the cooling of the indoor air, creating a comfortable and pleasant environment.

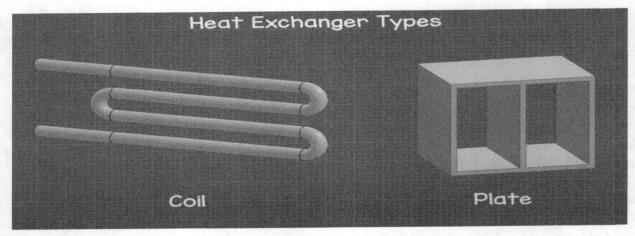

Figure 4.2 Evaporator Coil Types

Condenser Coil: Conversely, in the condenser coil, heat exchangers release heat absorbed from the indoor spaces into the outdoor environment. As the refrigerant changes from a high-pressure vapor to a high-pressure liquid, thermal energy is transferred to the outdoor air or a cooling medium, like water.

The design of heat exchangers involves maximizing surface area contact between the refrigerant and the surrounding air to enhance the efficiency of heat transfer. This is often achieved through the use of fins or ridges on the coil surfaces, which increase the surface area available for heat exchange.

Regular maintenance, including cleaning the coils and checking for any damage or blockages, is essential to ensure optimal heat transfer efficiency. Clean and well-maintained heat exchangers contribute to the overall performance and energy efficiency of the air conditioning system.

Fans:

Fans are fundamental components in air conditioning systems responsible for circulating air and ensuring proper airflow. They assist in moving air across the heat exchangers to facilitate the heat transfer process and distribute conditioned air throughout the building.

Blower Fan: The blower fan is part of the air handler or indoor unit and draws in indoor air from the return ducts. The air is then directed over the evaporator coils, where heat is absorbed, resulting in cooled air. The blower fan then circulates the cooled air back into the space through the supply ducts.

Condenser Fan: In the outdoor unit, the condenser fan works to dissipate the heat absorbed from the indoor spaces. It blows air over the condenser coils, facilitating the release of thermal energy to the outdoor environment or cooling medium.

Fans play a crucial role in achieving proper temperature control and comfort in indoor spaces. They ensure that conditioned air is effectively distributed throughout the building, maintaining a consistent and comfortable indoor climate.

Variable-Speed Fans: Some advanced air conditioning systems use variable-speed fans that adjust their speed based on the cooling demands. Variable-speed fans offer greater energy efficiency by optimizing airflow based on the specific cooling requirements of the system.

Refrigerant:

Refrigerant is a key component in air conditioning systems, responsible for absorbing and releasing heat during the cooling and heating processes. It undergoes phase changes from a low-pressure vapor to a high-pressure liquid and vice versa as it circulates through the system. Understanding the properties and selection of the appropriate refrigerant is essential for the proper functioning and efficiency of the air conditioning system.

Properties of Refrigerant: The ideal refrigerant possesses specific characteristics that make it suitable for air conditioning applications. These properties include low boiling points, high heat transfer capabilities, and chemical stability. Common refrigerants used in air conditioning systems include hydrofluorocarbons (HFCs), hydrochlorofluorocarbons (HCFCs), and hydrocarbons (HCs).

Phase Change: Refrigerant undergoes phase changes to absorb and release heat during the cooling process. In the evaporator, it changes from a low-pressure vapor to a low-pressure liquid while absorbing heat from the indoor air. In the condenser, it changes from a high-pressure vapor to a high-pressure liquid, releasing heat to the outdoor environment.

Refrigerant Selection: The selection of refrigerant is influenced by various factors, including energy efficiency, environmental impact, safety, and regulatory compliance. In recent years, there has been a transition towards using refrigerants with lower global warming potential (GWP) to mitigate their impact on climate change. As such, older refrigerants with higher ozone depletion potential (ODP) and GWP, such as chlorofluorocarbons (CFCs) and hydrochlorofluorocarbons (HCFCs), are being phased out and replaced with more environmentally friendly options, such as hydrofluorocarbons (HFCs) with lower GWP or natural refrigerants like hydrocarbons (HCs) and carbon dioxide (CO_2).

Thermostats:

Thermostats are crucial control devices in air conditioning systems, responsible for monitoring and regulating the indoor temperature. They provide users with the ability to set desired temperature levels, and the thermostat operates the air conditioning system to maintain those settings.

Operation and Control: Thermostats work by sensing the current indoor temperature and comparing it to the set temperature. When the indoor temperature deviates from the set value, the thermostat signals the air conditioning system to turn on or off to achieve the desired temperature. Some advanced thermostats may have additional features, such as programmable settings, Wi-Fi connectivity for remote control, and integration with smart home systems.

Types of Thermostats: There are various types of thermostats available for air conditioning systems, including:

Mechanical Thermostats: Mechanical thermostats are simple devices with a bimetallic coil that expands and contracts with temperature changes, triggering the on/off control of the system.

Digital Thermostats: Digital thermostats utilize electronic sensors and displays to provide precise temperature readings and easy-to-use controls.

Programmable Thermostats: Programmable thermostats allow users to set temperature schedules for different times of the day or week. This feature enables energy-saving by adjusting temperature settings during unoccupied periods.

Smart Thermostats: Smart thermostats are equipped with Wi-Fi connectivity and advanced features, allowing users to control the system remotely through mobile applications. They may also include smart sensors and algorithms to learn user preferences and optimize energy efficiency.

Thermostat Location: Proper thermostat placement is essential for accurate temperature sensing and efficient operation. Thermostats should be installed away from direct sunlight, drafts, and heat sources to ensure they provide a representative reading of the indoor temperature.

Run Capacitor:
The run capacitor is an essential electrical component in air conditioning systems, particularly in the operation of blower motors and compressors. Its primary function is to provide a phase shift to the electrical current, improving the efficiency and performance of the motors.

In the case of the blower motor, the run capacitor creates a phase difference between the main winding and the auxiliary winding, resulting in a rotating magnetic field. This rotating field enhances the torque and allows the blower motor to start and operate smoothly.

For compressors, the run capacitor plays a similar role, providing a phase shift to the current in the motor windings, which optimizes the motor's efficiency and allows it to run smoothly. Proper sizing and functioning of the run capacitor are essential for the efficient operation of the blower motor and compressor.

Blower Motor:
The blower motor is responsible for moving air through the air conditioning system, distributing conditioned air to different areas of the building. It is a vital component in ensuring proper airflow and providing comfort to occupants.

There are different types of blower motors used in air conditioning systems, including:

Single-Speed Motors: These motors have a fixed speed and operate at a constant airflow rate. They are commonly found in older air conditioning systems and provide a straightforward and reliable operation.

Multi-Speed Motors: Multi-speed blower motors offer the flexibility of operating at different speeds, allowing for adjustable airflow rates. They are often found in modern air conditioning systems and provide better control over indoor comfort.

Variable-Speed Motors: Variable-speed blower motors utilize advanced technology to offer infinite speed variations, allowing for precise and efficient control of airflow. These motors provide excellent energy efficiency and comfort.

Blower motors require regular maintenance, including lubrication and cleaning, to ensure their smooth operation and longevity.

Contactor:
The contactor is an electrical switch that controls the flow of electrical power to the compressor and the blower motor. It plays a vital role in starting and stopping these components.

When the thermostat signals the air conditioning system to start cooling, the contactor engages, allowing electrical power to flow to the compressor and blower motor. This starts the cooling process, and the air conditioning system begins to operate.

When the desired indoor temperature is reached or the thermostat signals the system to stop cooling, the contactor disengages, cutting off the electrical power to the compressor and blower motor. This stops the cooling process, and the system returns to its idle state.

Contactors should be inspected regularly for signs of wear, corrosion, or damage, and replaced if necessary, to ensure the reliable and safe operation of the air conditioning system.

In summary, the run capacitor, blower motor, and contactor are crucial components in air conditioning systems. The run capacitor provides a phase shift to improve the efficiency of the blower motor and compressor. The blower motor is responsible for moving air through the system, and its type determines the level of control over airflow. The contactor acts as an electrical switch, controlling the flow of power to the compressor and blower motor, enabling the system to start and stop efficiently. Proper maintenance and functioning of these components are essential for the reliable and efficient operation of the air conditioning system.

Air Distribution and Ductwork Design

Importance of proper Air Distribution
Proper air distribution is a crucial aspect of effective and efficient air conditioning systems. It ensures that conditioned air is evenly and efficiently delivered to every corner of the space, resulting in optimal comfort, indoor air quality, and energy efficiency. Let's explore the importance of proper air distribution in more detail.

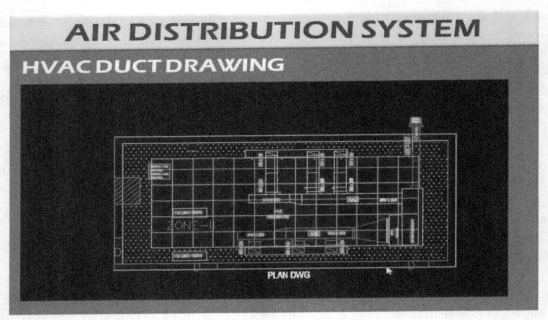

Figure 4.3 Air Distribution Drawing

Comfort and Indoor Air Quality:

Proper air distribution plays a significant role in maintaining comfortable indoor conditions. By distributing conditioned air evenly throughout the space, it helps to prevent temperature imbalances and hot or cold spots. This results in a consistent and comfortable environment for occupants.

Additionally, proper air distribution helps in maintaining adequate ventilation and air circulation, which is essential for indoor air quality. It ensures that fresh air is effectively mixed and distributed, helping to remove pollutants, odors, and excess humidity. This contributes to a healthier and more pleasant indoor environment.

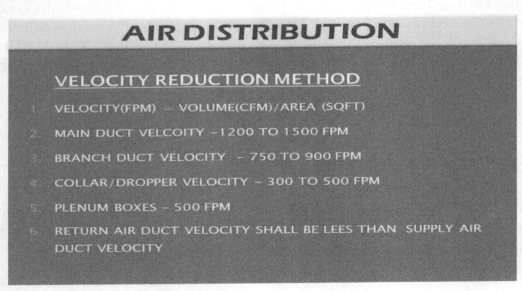

Figure 4.4 Efficient Air Distribution Reduction Method

Energy Efficiency:
Efficient air distribution reduces energy consumption and improves the overall energy efficiency of the air conditioning system. When conditioned air is properly distributed, it reaches the desired areas efficiently, minimizing the need for excessive cooling or heating. This reduces energy waste and lowers operating costs.

Proper air distribution also enables the air conditioning system to operate at optimal performance levels. It helps to maintain consistent airflow and temperature control, reducing the workload on the system. This results in improved energy efficiency and prolonged equipment life.

AIR DISTRIBUTION

DUCT PRESSURE CLASS	STATIC PRESSURE LIMIT		MAXIMUM AIR VELOCITY	PERMISSIBLE AIR LEAKAGE
	+ve	-ve		
	pa	pa	M/sec	Litters per sec per square meter
Low Pressure Class-A	500	500	10	$0.027 \times p^{0.65}$
Medium Pressure Class-B	1000	750	20	$0.009 \times p^{0.65}$
High Pressure Class-C	2000	750	40	$0.003 \times p^{0.65}$
Where p is in Pascal				

Figure 4.5 Balanced Load Distribution Pressure

Balanced Load Distribution:
Effective air distribution ensures that the cooling or heating load is evenly distributed across the space. It helps to balance the load between different zones or rooms, preventing overcooling or overheating in certain areas. This not only enhances comfort but also optimizes energy consumption by avoiding unnecessary conditioning of unoccupied or less frequently used spaces.

Noise Reduction:
Proper air distribution can help minimize noise levels in the indoor environment. By ensuring balanced airflow, it reduces the strain on the air conditioning system's fans and ductwork, resulting in quieter operation. This is particularly important in residential or commercial settings where noise control is essential for occupant comfort and productivity.

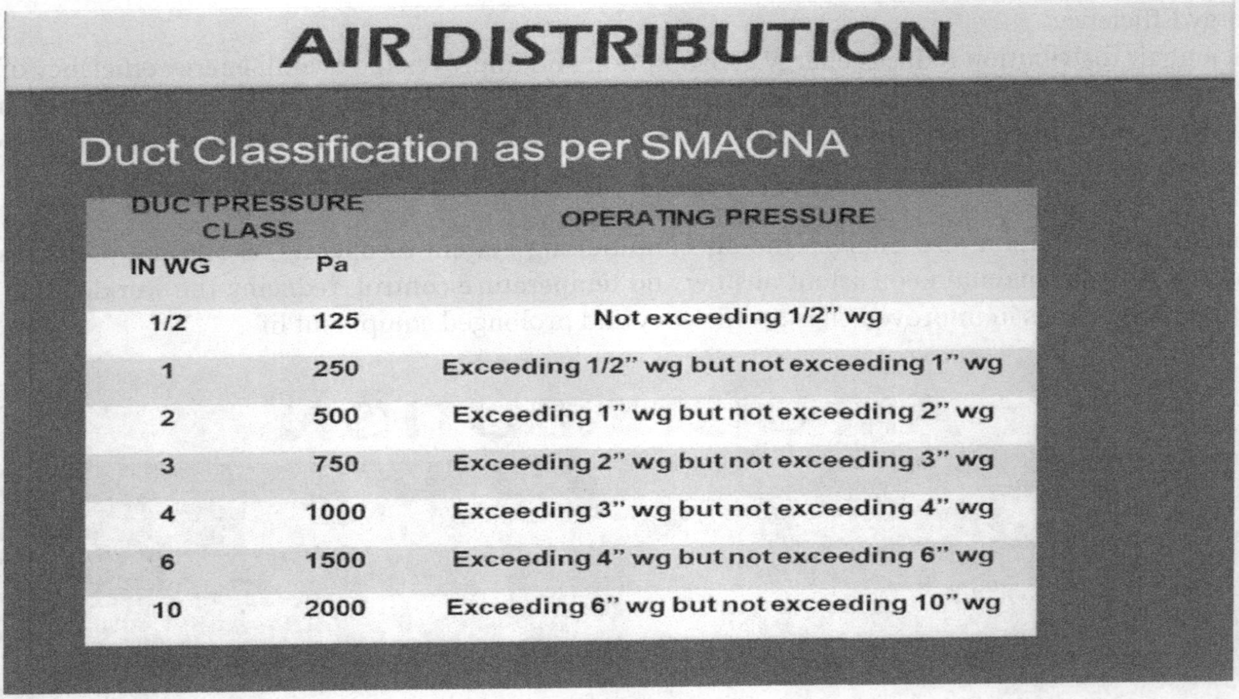

AIR DISTRIBUTION

Duct Classification as per SMACNA

DUCT PRESSURE CLASS		OPERATING PRESSURE
IN WG	Pa	
1/2	125	Not exceeding 1/2" wg
1	250	Exceeding 1/2" wg but not exceeding 1" wg
2	500	Exceeding 1" wg but not exceeding 2" wg
3	750	Exceeding 2" wg but not exceeding 3" wg
4	1000	Exceeding 3" wg but not exceeding 4" wg
6	1500	Exceeding 4" wg but not exceeding 6" wg
10	2000	Exceeding 6" wg but not exceeding 10" wg

Figure 4.6 Duct Classification

System Performance and Longevity:
Efficient air distribution contributes to the overall performance and longevity of the air conditioning system. When conditioned air is properly distributed, it reduces strain on the system's components, including the fan motor and compressor. This leads to improved reliability and reduced maintenance requirements, extending the lifespan of the system.

To achieve proper air distribution, careful ductwork design, including duct sizing, layout, and register placement, is necessary. Balancing airflow through dampers and adjusting air volume at diffusers or registers helps to fine-tune the distribution system.

Regular maintenance and inspections are also essential to ensure that ductwork remains clean, free from leaks, and properly insulated. Any obstructions, leaks, or imbalances should be addressed promptly to maintain optimal air distribution.

Types of Ductwork Materials
Ductwork is an integral part of air conditioning systems, responsible for delivering conditioned air from the central unit to various spaces within a building. Ductwork materials play a crucial role in determining the efficiency, durability, and overall performance of the air distribution system. Let's explore some common types of ductwork materials used in air conditioning systems:

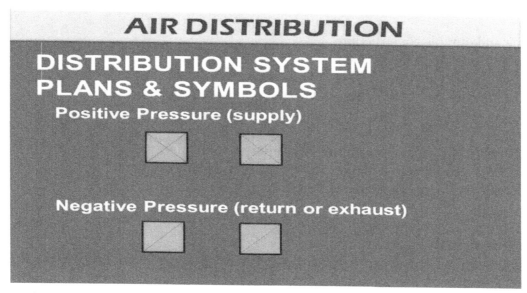

Figure 4.7 Air Distribution Positive & Negative Pressure Symbols

Sheet Metal

Sheet metal ductwork, typically made of galvanized steel, is one of the most common and durable options available. It offers excellent structural integrity, allowing for smooth airflow and minimal air leakage. Sheet metal ducts are suitable for both residential and commercial applications and can be customized to fit specific design requirements.

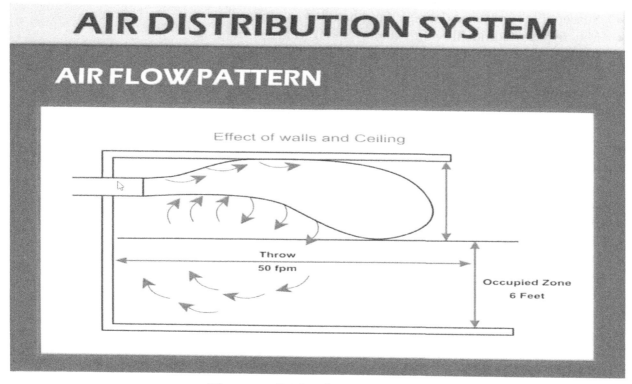

Figure 4.8 Air Flow Direction

Advantages
- Strong and durable construction
- Resistant to damage, pests, and fire
- Provides smooth airflow
- Can be insulated for better energy efficiency and noise reduction

Disadvantages
- Can be relatively expensive compared to other materials
- Requires professional installation and fabrication skills
- Prone to corrosion if not adequately protected

Fiberglass Ductboard
Fiberglass ductboard is a type of pre-insulated ductwork material made of fiberglass-reinforced panels. It is lightweight, easy to handle, and offers good thermal insulation properties. Fiberglass ductboard is commonly used in residential applications and low-pressure HVAC systems.

Advantages:
- Lightweight and easy to install
- Provides built-in insulation
- Resistant to moisture and mold growth
- Offers good acoustic insulation properties

Disadvantages
- Susceptible to physical damage if not handled carefully
- May require additional sealing to prevent air leakage
- Limited to low-pressure applications

Flexible Ducts
Flexible ducts consist of a flexible plastic inner core surrounded by insulation and an outer protective layer. They are flexible and easy to install, making them suitable for applications where space is limited or when navigating around obstacles. Flexible ducts are commonly used in residential and light commercial HVAC systems.

Advantages
- Highly flexible and easy to install
- Ideal for retrofit or hard-to-reach areas
- Provides built-in insulation
- Reduces noise transmission

Figure 4.9 HVAC Control Systems

Disadvantages
- More susceptible to airflow restrictions and pressure loss
- Prone to kinks and bends if not properly supported
- Can be more challenging to clean and maintain

Duct Board
Duct board, also known as rigid fiberglass duct, is made of fiberglass panels bonded together to form a solid duct. It offers good thermal insulation properties and is often used in commercial applications where higher temperature and pressure requirements exist.

Advantages
- Provides excellent thermal insulation
- Resistant to moisture, pests, and mold growth
- Suitable for higher temperature and pressure applications

Disadvantages
- Can be relatively expensive
- Requires proper sealing and insulation to prevent air leakage
- Challenging to modify or repair once installed

PVC and Flexible Plastic Ducts
PVC (polyvinyl chloride) and flexible plastic ducts are lightweight and affordable options for air distribution systems. They are commonly used in portable or temporary cooling applications, such as construction sites or event spaces.

Advantages
- Lightweight and cost-effective
- Easy to install and modify

- Suitable for temporary or portable applications

Disadvantages
- Limited durability compared to other materials
- Can be more susceptible to damage and air leakage
- Not suitable for high-temperature or high-pressure applications

The selection of ductwork material depends on various factors, including the specific application, budget, design requirements, and system performance expectations. Consulting with a professional HVAC contractor or engineer can help determine the most suitable ductwork material for your specific needs, ensuring optimal airflow, energy efficiency, and comfort in your air conditioning system.

Duct Insulation and Sealing Techniques
Proper insulation and sealing of ductwork are essential for maintaining the efficiency, performance, and energy savings of air conditioning systems. Insulation helps prevent heat gain or loss in the ducts, while sealing ensures that conditioned air reaches its intended destination without leakage. Let's explore some common duct insulation and sealing techniques used in air distribution systems:

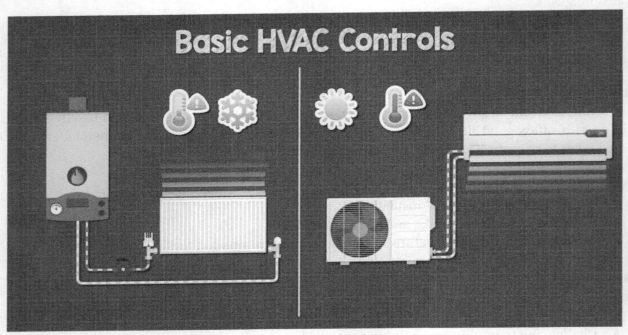

Figure 4.10 Duct Insulation of Outdoor and Indoor Unit

Duct Insulation:
Duct insulation is crucial for minimizing heat transfer between the conditioned air inside the ducts and the surrounding environment. It helps maintain the desired temperature of the air and reduces energy losses. Common insulation materials used for ductwork include fiberglass, foam board, and reflective insulation.

Insulating ductwork provides several benefits:

Energy Efficiency: Insulated ducts minimize thermal losses or gains, reducing the energy required to heat or cool the air.

Improved Comfort: Insulation helps maintain the desired temperature of the air, preventing hot or cold spots and enhancing overall comfort.

Condensation Control: Insulation reduces the likelihood of condensation forming on the exterior of the ducts, minimizing the risk of moisture-related issues such as mold growth.

Noise Reduction: Insulated ducts help reduce noise transmission from the HVAC system, resulting in a quieter indoor environment.

When insulating ductwork, it is important to consider the appropriate insulation thickness, which depends on factors such as climate, duct location, and desired energy efficiency. Consulting local building codes or working with a professional HVAC contractor can help determine the appropriate insulation requirements for your specific application.

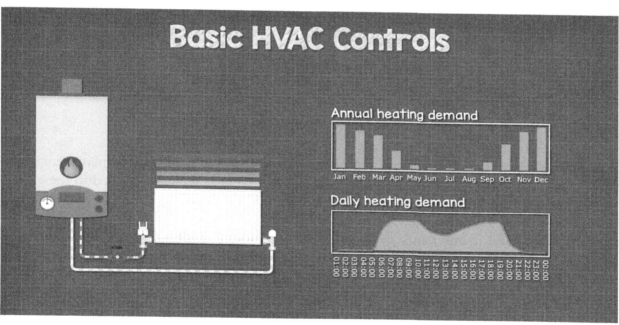

Figure 4.11 Annual and Daily Heating Demand

Duct Sealing:

Proper sealing of ductwork is crucial to prevent air leakage, which can result in energy waste, reduced system performance, and compromised indoor air quality. Here are some effective duct sealing techniques:

Mastic Sealant: Mastic is a flexible sealant that is applied to the joints, seams, and connections of ductwork. It provides an airtight seal and helps prevent air leakage. Mastic can be brushed or applied using a caulking gun.

Foil Tape: Foil tape is a durable, heat-resistant tape used to seal duct joints and connections. It adheres well to metal surfaces and provides an effective barrier against air leakage.

Aeroseal: Aeroseal is a specialized duct sealing method that involves injecting a sealant into the ductwork. The sealant circulates within the ducts and seals any leaks or gaps, improving overall duct efficiency. Aeroseal is typically performed by trained professionals.

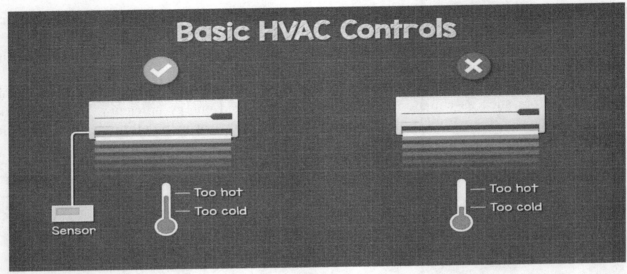

Figure 4.12 HVAC Hot and Cold Sensors

Duct Insulation Wrap: In addition to insulating the ducts, wrapping them with insulation material can help improve sealing and minimize air leakage. Insulation wrap is typically applied to the exterior of the ducts and helps reduce heat transfer and condensation.

Regular inspection and maintenance of ductwork are important to identify and address any leaks or damaged sections promptly. Properly sealed and insulated ductwork ensures that conditioned air is delivered efficiently, reducing energy consumption, improving system performance, and maintaining desired indoor comfort.

Air Conditioning System Controls and Thermostats

Control Systems and Thermostats in HVAC:
Control systems are indispensable for managing and regulating air conditioning systems to achieve desired comfort levels, energy efficiency, and overall operational effectiveness. These intricate systems encompass a diverse array of components, functioning collaboratively to monitor, control, and adjust the operation of HVAC systems. Here, we provide a succinct overview of the technical aspects of control systems in air conditioning:

Thermostats:
Thermostats serve as the principal user interface for temperature control within a space. These instrumental devices empower occupants to modulate desired temperature settings and furnish input to the control system. Contemporary thermostats boast advanced attributes like programmable

scheduling, occupancy sensing, and remote accessibility, thus imparting augmented control capabilities and energy-saving potential.

Sensors:
Sensors are pivotal for collecting environmental data within the space or about the HVAC system itself. Common sensor types include temperature sensors, humidity sensors, occupancy sensors, and air quality sensors. These sensors furnish feedback to the control system, enabling informed decision-making and responsive adjustments.

Controllers:
Controllers assimilate input from sensors and thermostats, deploying programmed logic or algorithms to effectuate decisions. Communication with various HVAC system components, such as compressors, fans, and damper actuators, facilitates precise regulation of the system's operation. Controllers may manifest as standalone entities or be integrated into more sophisticated building automation systems (BAS).

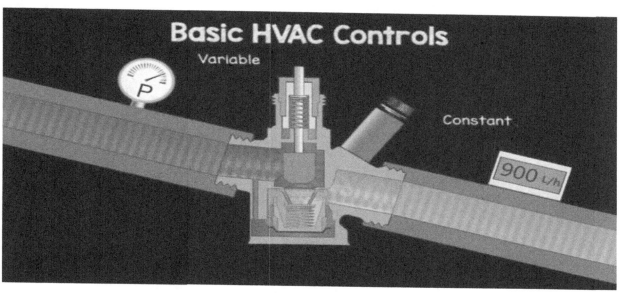

Figure 4.13 Actuators execute control

Actuators:
Actuators execute control commands issued by controllers, tangibly adjusting the operation of HVAC components. They effectuate functions such as modulating airflow through dampers, varying fan or pump speeds, or controlling valve positions. Actuators ensure the effective implementation of designated control settings.

Building Automation Systems (BAS):
Building Automation Systems engender the seamless coordination and unification of various building systems, including HVAC, lighting, security, etc. By furnishing centralized control and monitoring, BAS empowers the deployment of advanced strategies, such as demand-based control, occupancy scheduling, and energy optimization. These systems proffer heightened efficiency, comfort, and operational simplicity for larger and more intricate buildings.

Communication and Networking:
Control systems predominantly leverage diverse communication protocols and networks, facilitating coherent interaction between various components and devices. This enables remote access, monitoring, and centralized control. Commonly utilized protocols encompass BACnet, Modbus, LonWorks, and Internet of Things (IoT) technologies.

Control systems wield a decisive influence on maintaining optimal comfort, energy efficiency, and system performance in air conditioning applications. By continuously scrutinizing environmental conditions, assimilating occupant input, and promptly effecting adjustments, these systems harmonize to ensure a comfortable and sustainable indoor milieu.

Thermostats and their Functions:
Thermostats are pivotal components within air conditioning systems, empowering users to regulate and adjust temperature settings within a space. They discharge several vital functions:

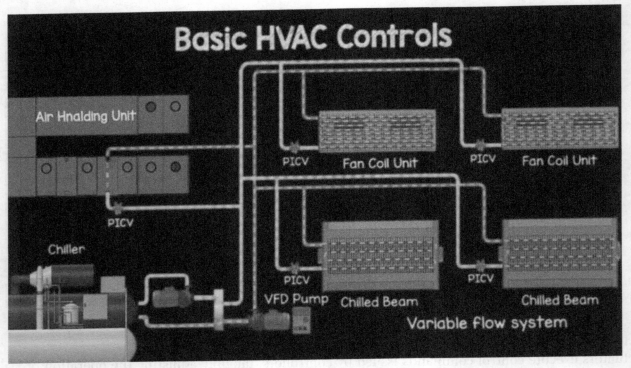

Figure 4.14 Temperature Control Variable Flow System

Temperature Control:
Foremost, thermostats execute the central task of regulating temperature within a building or room. Users establish their desired temperature, whereupon the thermostat instructs the HVAC system to adapt heating or cooling outputs correspondingly. This entails the perpetuation of comfort by upholding a consistent temperature level.

User Interface:

Thermostats provide the interface through which users interact with the HVAC system. Commonly equipped with digital or analog displays and buttons or touch controls, they afford users the ability to manipulate temperature settings, choose operational modes (heating, cooling, automatic), and configure scheduling options.

Programmable Schedules:
Many thermostats incorporate programmable scheduling functionality, empowering users to establish temperature adjustments based on specific times or days of the week. Such a feature optimizes energy usage by automatizing temperature modulation during unoccupied periods or specific time frames, such as occupants' sleep hours.

Energy Efficiency:
Thermostats constitute a pivotal instrument for promoting energy efficiency. By enabling users to establish temperature preferences and schedules, they effectively minimize energy consumption, ensuring the HVAC system operates solely when necessary. Smart thermostats even learn user behavioral patterns, autonomously adapting temperature settings for further energy conservation.

Sensor Inputs:
Thermostats incorporate a plethora of sensors for gathering intelligence about the indoor environment. Common sensor types encompass temperature sensors, humidity sensors, and occupancy sensors. These inputs enable thermostats to make astute decisions and adjustments based on prevailing conditions within the space.

Remote Access and Connectivity:
Advanced thermostats oftentimes offer remote access and connectivity features. Through mobile apps or web interfaces, users can control and monitor their HVAC systems from remote locations. Real-time adjustments, energy monitoring, and notifications are thereby facilitated, augmenting convenience and control.

Thermostats manifest in sundry types, spanning basic manual thermostats to programmable thermostats and advanced smart thermostats. Thermostat selection hinges upon user preferences, desired functionalities, and budgetary considerations.

Programmable and Smart Thermostats:
Programmable and smart thermostats constitute advanced control devices conferring augmented functionalities and energy-saving capabilities compared to traditional thermostats. Here, we provide an overview of programmable and smart thermostats:

Programmable Thermostats:
Programmable thermostats empower users to craft temperature schedules that reflect their preferences and occupancy patterns. In so doing, they preclude superfluous cooling or heating when the space remains unoccupied, yielding energy savings.

Energy Efficiency Benefits:

Programmable thermostats, through automated temperature adjustments based on preset schedules, optimize energy consumption. This ameliorates energy waste by circumventing needless cooling or heating when occupants are absent. Consequentially, programmable thermostats engender noteworthy energy savings and curtail utility expenses.

Smart Thermostats:

Smart thermostats elevate energy management and convenience to a higher echelon. These devices boast supplementary attributes, such as remote accessibility, learning capabilities, and seamless integration with home automation systems. Via smartphone apps or web interfaces, users can exercise real-time control and energy tracking.

Learning Algorithms:

Smart thermostats possess the capacity to "learn" from user behaviors, autonomously adapting temperature settings in response. By analyzing occupancy patterns, preferred temperatures, and sundry other factors, smart thermostats establish personalized schedules. Over time, they adeptly adapt to occupants' routines, optimizing comfort and energy efficiency sans manual intervention.

Sensor Integration:

Smart thermostats often incorporate an array of sensors beyond temperature sensors. Occupancy sensors, humidity sensors, and ambient light sensors, among others, intermingle to enable the thermostat to make informed decisions about temperature adjustments based on prevailing conditions.

Energy Monitoring and Reporting:

Numerous smart thermostats feature energy monitoring and reporting capabilities, empowering users to scrutinize their energy usage patterns and identify inefficiencies. By furnishing energy consumption data, energy-saving guidance, and monthly reports, users can render more informed decisions to optimize their HVAC systems' efficiency.

Integration with Home Automation:

Smart thermostats lend themselves to seamless integration with home automation systems, endowing users with coherent control over multiple smart devices. Voice assistants like Amazon Alexa or Google Assistant further supplement the user experience by enabling thermostat control through voice commands, thereby augmenting convenience and accessibility.

Control Wiring and Troubleshooting:

Control wiring is instrumental in effecting the linkage and coordination of various components within an air conditioning system. Its operation facilitates communication between thermostats, controllers, actuators, and other devices, thereby ensuring proper system functioning. Below, we furnish an abridged overview of control wiring and troubleshooting:

A Simplified BAS Architecture Example

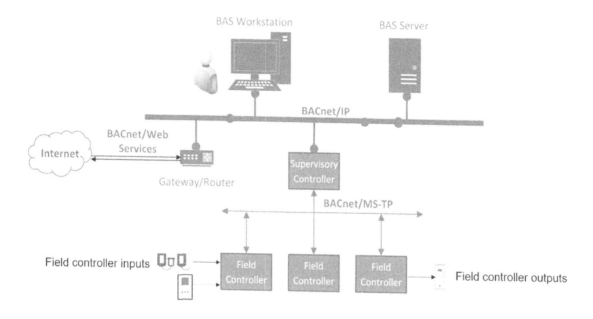

Figure 4.16 Integration with Home Automation

Control Wiring:

Control wiring comprises electrical connections that interconnect the thermostat, controllers, and actuators within the HVAC system. These connections enable signal and power transmission amid diverse components, engendering control and coordination. Typically low-voltage wiring is utilized in control wiring, as it imparts enhanced safety and ease of handling compared to high-voltage electrical wiring.

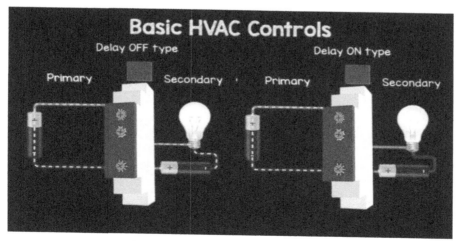

Figure 4.17 Wiring Diagrams

Wiring Diagrams:

Wiring diagrams visually depict control wiring connections in an air conditioning system. Illustrating components, terminals, and wire paths, wiring diagrams are indispensable references during installation, maintenance, and troubleshooting endeavors.

Troubleshooting:

Control wiring troubleshooting entails the identification and resolution of issues that impede communication and hinder the HVAC system's proper functioning. Common control wiring predicaments comprise loose or disconnected wires, faulty connections, damaged cables, or misconfigured wiring setups. Troubleshooting may necessitate the use of a multimeter or other testing equipment to verify continuity, voltage, and optimal wiring performance.

Safety Protocols:

During control wiring troubleshooting, stringent safety protocols must be adhered to. Power sources must be deactivated, and electrical components handled with meticulous care. Should the issue exceed one's expertise, it is advisable to seek assistance from a qualified HVAC technician or electrician.

Testing and Repair:

Upon identifying the source of a control wiring problem, requisite repairs or replacements are executed. This might encompass reestablishing loose connections, rectifying damaged cables, replacing faulty components, or correcting wiring errors. Subsequent testing of the system post-repairs is imperative to ensure proper functionality and ascertain accurate transmission of control signals.

Regular maintenance and inspection of control wiring contribute to preempting issues and ensuring dependable operation of the air conditioning system. Periodically verifying connections for looseness, inspecting wires for wear and tear, or scrutinizing signs of damage enables early detection of potential problems, precluding the advent of more severe issues.

Energy Management and Efficiency Strategies:

Energy management and efficiency strategies wield critical import in optimizing air conditioning system performance and mitigating energy consumption. Implementation of these strategies confers cost savings, enhances environmental sustainability, and improves system efficiency. Below, we provide a concise overview of energy management and efficiency strategies:

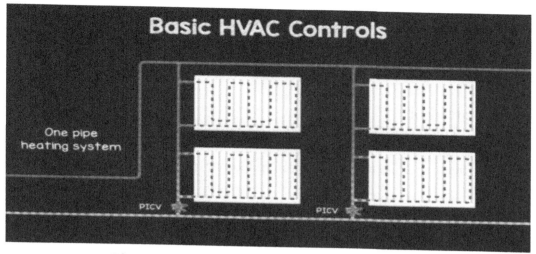

Figure 4.18 Variable Speed Drives Control

Programmable Thermostats:

Embracing programmable thermostats empowers users to devise temperature schedules that conform to occupancy patterns. This, in turn, curtails needless cooling or heating during unoccupied periods, curtailing energy waste and diminishing utility expenses.

Temperature Setbacks:

Temperature setbacks involve adjusting thermostat settings to marginally higher temperatures during cooling or slightly lower temperatures during heating when spaces remain unoccupied or during times of decreased demand. This measure effectuates energy conservation without compromising comfort.

Zoning Systems:

Zoning systems partition buildings into separate zones, each with autonomous temperature control. Such systems direct conditioned air solely to occupied areas, minimizing energy waste in unoccupied zones while conferring customized comfort for distinct areas.

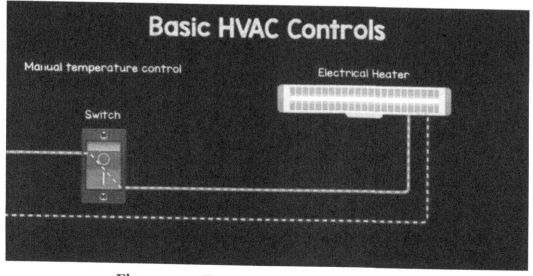

Figure 4.19 Temperature Control Switch

Variable Speed Drives:
Fans and pump motors in HVAC equipment are outfitted with variable speed drives (VSDs) to modulate their speed in response to demand. This feature facilitates energy modulation, as power consumption diminishes during low-demand periods, while overall system efficiency is enhanced.

Energy Recovery Ventilation:
Energy recovery ventilation (ERV) systems recover and exchange heat or humidity between incoming and outgoing airstreams. This process mitigates the workload on cooling and heating systems, promoting energy efficiency while upholding fresh indoor air quality.

Regular Maintenance:
Periodic maintenance of air conditioning systems is pivotal for optimal performance and energy efficiency. Tasks such as air filter cleaning or replacement, coil inspection and cleaning, and maintenance of proper refrigerant levels contribute to efficient operation and improved energy management.

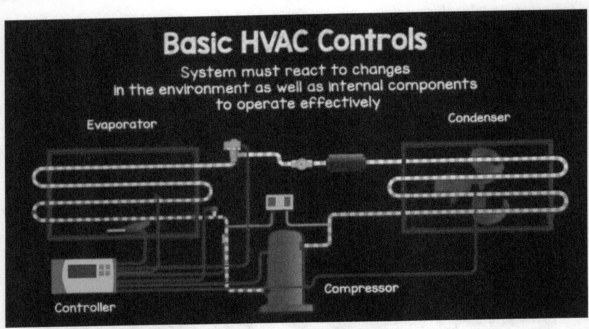

Figure 4.20 Energy Recovery Ventilation

Air Leakage Reduction:
Sealing air leaks in ductwork and around windows and doors curtails the loss of conditioned air and the intrusion of outdoor air. Proper insulation and sealing techniques uphold desired indoor temperatures, diminish energy waste, and augment comfort.

Energy Monitoring and Analytics:
Employment of energy monitoring systems and analytics software allows users to scrutinize and analyze energy consumption patterns, recognizing inefficiencies and effectuating data-driven decisions to optimize energy management and system performance.

Book 5

Heating Systems and Technologies

Introduction to Heating Systems

Heating systems play a crucial role in creating comfortable indoor environments, especially during colder months. Whether it's a residential, commercial, or industrial setting, understanding the basics of heating systems is essential for anyone interested in mastering HVAC systems. In this chapter, we will provide an introduction to heating systems, exploring their significance and the various technologies involved.

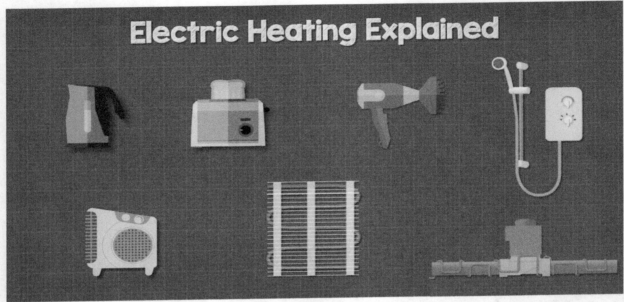

Figure 5.1 Heating Systems and Appliances

Understanding the Importance of Heating Systems

Heating systems serve the primary purpose of maintaining desirable indoor temperatures, ensuring warmth and comfort for occupants. They are vital for creating a pleasant living or working environment, allowing individuals to stay productive, healthy, and safe even when the weather outside is chilly.

In addition to comfort, heating systems are essential for protecting buildings and their contents from the detrimental effects of extreme cold. They prevent issues such as frozen pipes, condensation, and structural damage caused by temperature fluctuations. Heating systems also contribute to maintaining proper humidity levels, which further enhances comfort and prevents issues related to excessive dryness.

Overview of Different Heating Technologies

Heating systems employ a variety of technologies to generate and distribute heat throughout a space. Understanding these technologies will provide a foundation for exploring the specific types of heating systems in greater detail.

Furnaces

One of the most popular heating methods, particularly in homes, is the furnace. To produce heat, they require fuel such as oil, propane, or natural gas. Using ducting and vents, the warm air is then dispersed throughout the building.

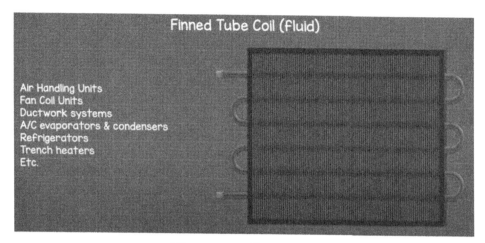

Figure 5.2 Furnaces

Boilers

Heat is transferred through water or steam in boilers. By burning fuel, they heat water or create steam, which is then sent to radiators, baseboard heaters, or underfloor pipes to warm the room. Residential and commercial buildings frequently have boilers, which are renowned for their effectiveness.

Heat Pumps

Heat pumps are versatile heating systems that can also provide cooling. They extract heat from the outdoor air, ground, or water sources and transfer it indoors. Heat pumps can operate in reverse during warmer months, effectively cooling the space. This technology offers energy efficiency and is gaining popularity in both residential and commercial applications.

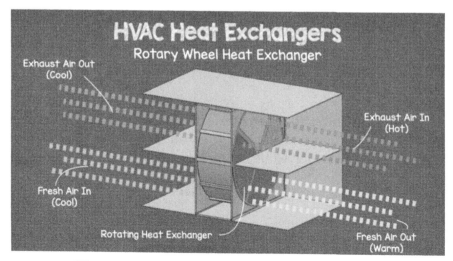

Figure 5.3 Rotary Wheel Heat Exchanger

Radiant Heating Systems
Radiant heating systems involve the direct transfer of heat to objects and surfaces within a space, rather than heating the air. This can be achieved through electric radiant systems, hydronic (water-based) systems, or even radiant panels embedded in walls or floors. Radiant heating offers a comfortable and efficient heating solution.

Geothermal Heating Systems
Geothermal heating systems utilize the stable temperature of the ground or groundwater as a heat source. They transfer this heat to the building using a ground loop system and a heat pump. Geothermal systems provide excellent energy efficiency and are environmentally friendly.

By familiarizing ourselves with the importance of heating systems and the various technologies employed, we can delve deeper into specific heating system types, their components, installation techniques, maintenance considerations, and energy-saving strategies. Let's explore forced-air heating systems, hydronic heating systems, and electric heating systems in the following chapters to gain a comprehensive understanding of heating technologies.

Forced-Air Heating Systems

Forced-air heating systems, renowned for their swift and efficient heat distribution, find widespread application in residential, commercial, and industrial settings. This segment delves into the intricate mechanics of forced-air heating systems, encompassing their operational principles, constituent elements, installation nuances, and maintenance proclivities.

Mechanisms of Forced-Air Heating Systems:
At the crux of a forced-air heating system resides either a furnace or a heat pump. The furnace proffers heat by means of fuel combustion (such as natural gas, propane, or oil) or via electric resistance heating. In contrast, the heat pump extracts heat from outdoor air, the ground, or water sources. Post heat generation or extraction, a blower or fan impels the warmed air through an extensive network of ductwork, disbursing it into diverse chambers or zones.

Components of Forced-Air Heating Systems:
Forced-air heating systems are conglomerations of key components, harmoniously functioning to furnish warmth and comfort across the edifice:

.Furnace or Heat Pump:
The furnace or heat pump constitutes the epicenter of the forced-air heating system. It initiates heat generation or harnesses environmental heat, contingent on the system type. Furnaces conventionally utilize natural gas, propane, or oil as fuel, while heat pumps employ electricity to propel heat transfer.

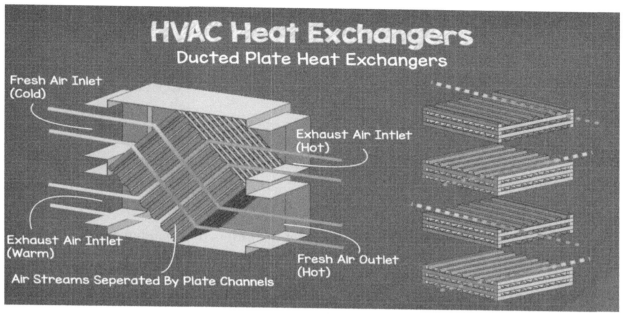

Figure 5.4 Forced-Air Duct Plate Heat Exchanger

Ductwork:
Ductwork constitutes the distribution medium for heated air. Comprising a series of metal or flexible tubes that originate from the furnace or heat pump, ducts traverse various sections of the edifice. Dampers and registers regulate airflow, directing heat toward specified zones.

Air Handlers:
Air handlers actuate air movement through the ductwork. Equipped with blowers or fans, they draw air from the return ducts, propel it across the heat exchanger (in furnace systems), and subsequently force it into the supply ducts for dissemination.

Air Filters and Purifiers:
Forced-air systems are graced with air filters that purge the circulating air of dust, allergens, and other particulates. Air purifiers may be appended to elevate indoor air quality by curbing contaminants and ameliorating respiratory health.

Thermostats and Controls:
Thermostats preside over temperature regulation, discerning the present temperature and adapting heating operations accordingly. Advanced thermostats may be programmed to comply with predetermined schedules, fostering energy-efficient temperature control. Controls may entail zoning systems that segment the edifice into distinct temperature zones, ushering in individualized climate control.

Installation and Sizing Prerequisites:
Installation mandates meticulous deliberation regarding furnace or heat pump sizing to yield optimal heating performance. Building dimensions, insulation, and climate idiosyncrasies factor into the sizing

97

calculus. Prudent sizing precludes superfluous energy consumption or inadequacies in heating capacity.

Further, the ductwork's design and installation hold prime significance for efficient heat dissemination. Proper duct sealing and insulation forestall heat dissipation and ensure seamless airflow.

Operation and Maintenance Guidelines:
Maintaining forced-air heating system proficiency and efficiency hails through regular maintenance. Essential tips encompass:

Cleaning and Replacing Air Filters:
Air filters necessitate periodic cleaning or replacement to forestall dust buildup and uphold indoor air quality. Clogged filters impede airflow, impairing system efficiency.

Duct Inspection and Cleaning:
Periodic ductwork scrutiny and cleaning obviate dirt, debris, and obstructions that impede airflow. Pristine ducts amplify air quality and optimize heat dissemination.

Troubleshooting Common Issues:
Grasping prevalent issues like ignition hitches, thermostat malfunctions, or blower motor failures facilitates resolution of minor predicaments. However, complex issues warrant professional technician consultation.

Energy Efficiency Enhancement Strategies:
Endorsing energy-saving practices, such as programmable thermostats, adequate insulation, air leak sealing, and systematic system maintenance, heightens the energy efficiency of forced-air heating systems, curtailing utility costs and environmental impact.

Forced-air heating systems epitomize a versatile and efficacious heating modality. Through cogent comprehension of their elements, installation prerequisites, and maintenance imperatives, stakeholders can optimize system performance, ensuring cozy and efficient heating throughout abodes or workplaces.

Hydronic Heating Systems

Hydronic heating systems epitomize efficient and comfortable heating mechanisms, leveraging water or steam as the conduits for heat transfer. Predominantly employed in residential and commercial settings, these systems yield manifold benefits, such as uniform heat dispersion, unobtrusive operation, and versatile design adaptability. This segment delves into the intricate mechanics of hydronic heating systems, encompassing their operational principles, constituents, installation nuances, and maintenance proclivities.

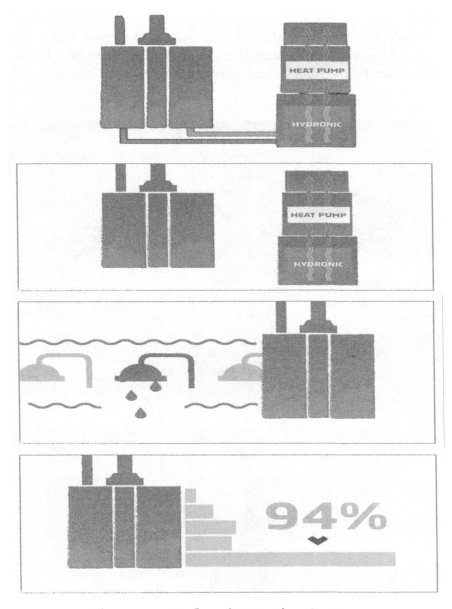

Figure 5.5 Hydronic Heating Systems

Hydronic Heating System Mechanics:

Hydronic heating systems function by heating water or generating steam, subsequently disseminating it through an intricate network of pipes to liberate heat into the ambient surroundings. This heat exchange occurs via diverse methods, inclusive of radiators, baseboard heaters, or underfloor pipes. Following the heat transfer process, the cooled water or steam circulates back to the heating source for reheating, establishing an uninterrupted cycle of comforting warmth.

Constituents of a Hydronic Heating System:

A hydronic heating system manifests as an amalgamation of pivotal components, synergistically cooperating to furnish efficient and gratifying warmth:

Boiler or Water Heater:

The epicenter of a hydronic heating system resides in the boiler or water heater. This cardinal apparatus employs a fuel source, such as natural gas, propane, or oil, to heat water or generate steam. Boilers are available in manifold variants, encompassing conventional boilers, condensing boilers, and combi boilers.

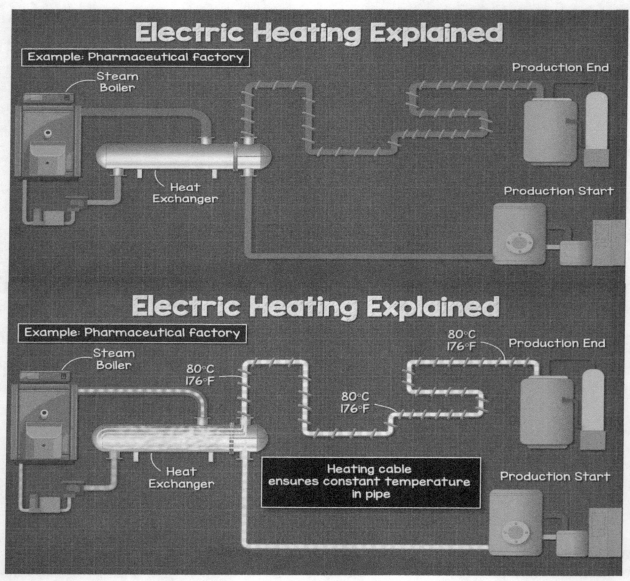

Figure 5.6 Boiler or Water Heater Exchanger

Radiators and Baseboard Heaters:

Radiators and baseboard heaters surface as the most prevalent heat emitters in hydronic systems. Radiators are metallic units adorned with fins or tubes that effectuate heat liberation via convection. Conversely, baseboard heaters, elongated and slender units nestled along the base of walls, furnish radiant heat.

Piping and Valves:

The conveyance of heated water or steam transpires via piping from the boiler to the heat emitters and back. Prominent materials employed for piping entail steel, cross-linked polyethylene, or copper. Valves come into play to regulate temperature and steam or water flow across diverse areas of the structure.

Expansion Tanks and Pressure Relief Valves:

Expansion tanks acclimate the expansion of heated water within the system, preserving consistent pressure levels. Pressure relief valves act as safety measures, liberating excess pressure from the system to avert damages.

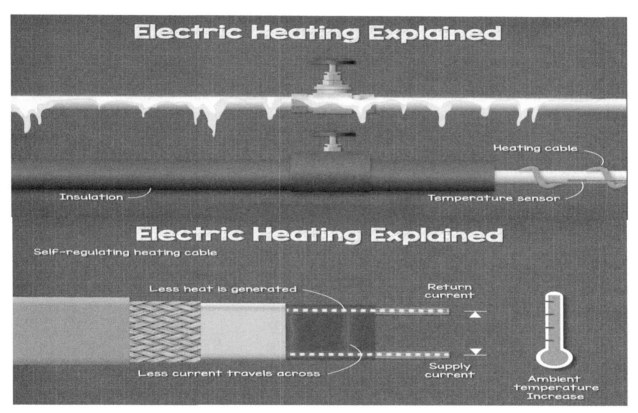

Figure 5.7 Regulate Temperatures Controls

Controls and Thermostats:

Controls and thermostats furnish users with the capability to regulate temperatures within distinct zones or rooms. Bestowing flexibility in managing heating requisites, these entities can be programmed to modify temperatures in accordance with occupancy or time of day.

Installation and Sizing Prerequisites:

Adequate installation is a sine qua non for hydronic heating system efficacy and efficiency. Pertinent factors, such as heat load calculations, pipe sizing, and emitter selection, warrant thorough contemplation. Professional installation engenders optimal performance and comfort while circumventing potential conundrums such as non-uniform heat dispersion or inadequate heating capacity.

Operation and Maintenance Guidelines:
Regular maintenance is indispensable to ensure hydronic heating system efficiency and endurance. Essential tips encompass:

Water Treatment and Maintenance:
Prudent water treatment forestalls corrosion and scale buildup within the system. Periodic maintenance encompasses boiler inspection and upkeep, pressure level assessments, and expeditious leakage resolution.

Balancing Hydronic Systems:
Balancing entails flow rate adjustments in diverse zones to attain uniform heat dispersion. This facilitates the commensurate allocation of heat to each region, mitigating undue heat exertion or underutilization of specific heat emitters.

Troubleshooting Common Issues:
Familiarizing oneself with prevalent issues such as airlocks, pump malfunctions, or thermostat irregularities streamlines the process of troubleshooting and remedying minor quandaries. Complex matters necessitate the counsel of a skilled technician.

Energy Efficiency Enhancement Strategies:
Implementing energy-conserving practices, such as programmable thermostats, insulation installation, and systematic system upkeep, augments hydronic heating system energy efficiency, thereby curtailing energy consumption and expenses.

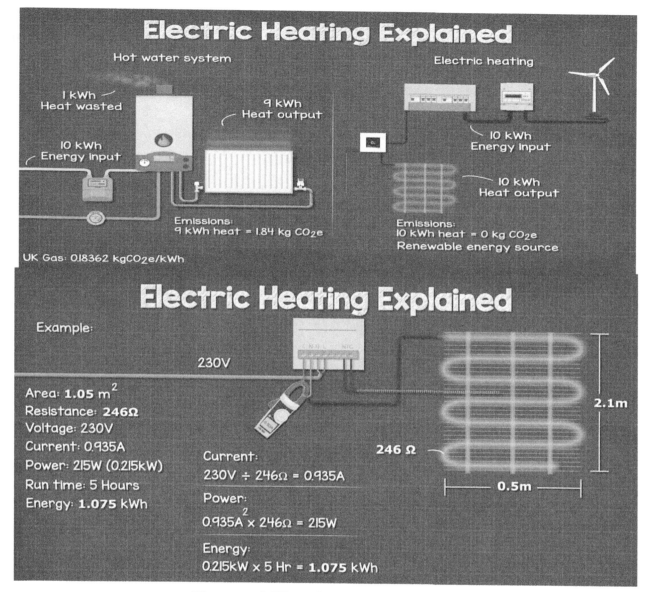

Figure 5.8 Electric Heating Systems

Hydronic heating systems offer steadfast and proficient heating solutions, replete with superior comfort and control. Grasping the mechanics of their components, installation imperatives, and maintenance prerequisites empowers stakeholders to savor the multifarious benefits of this versatile heating system within residential and commercial edifices.

Electric Heating Systems

Electric heating systems present a direct and expedient heating solution for residential and commercial applications. Leveraging electrical energy for heat generation, these systems proficiently deliver warmth and comfort. This segment delves into the fundamental mechanics of electric heating systems, encompassing diverse types, operational principles, installation requisites, and maintenance guidelines.

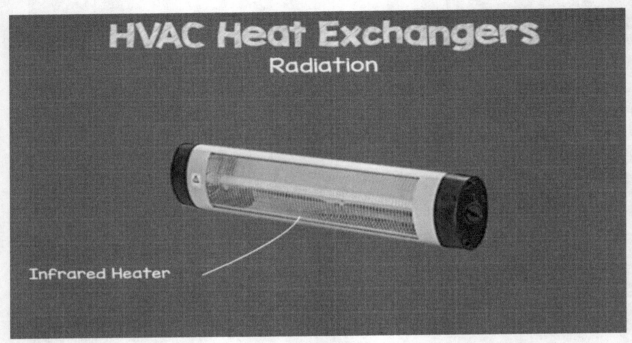

Figure 5.9 Electrical Resistance Heating Elements

Types of Electric Heating Systems:
Electric heating systems manifest in a multiplicity of types, tailored to specific applications and preferences. Notable varieties encompass:

Electric Furnaces:
Electric furnaces harness electrical resistance heating elements, typically coiled wires. As electric current courses through these elements, they undergo heating, disseminating warm air via blowers throughout the space.

Electric Baseboard Heaters:
Baseboard heaters feature heating elements enclosed within metal housing, installed along wall bases. As electric current courses through these elements, they emit radiant heat, warming the surrounding air. Individual thermostats often govern baseboard heaters, enabling zonal temperature control.

Electric Radiant Heating:
Electric radiant heating systems feature electric cables or mats installed beneath floors, walls, or ceilings. These heating elements generate radiant heat, directly warming objects and surfaces. Electric radiant heating proves efficacious and comfortable, especially in areas with tile or stone flooring.

Electric Heating System Operation:
Electric heating systems execute heat generation by transforming electrical energy into heat energy via resistance heating. Heating elements, whether in furnaces or radiant systems, impede electric current flow, inducing heating. The ensuing heat transfer to the surrounding air or objects effectuates space warming.

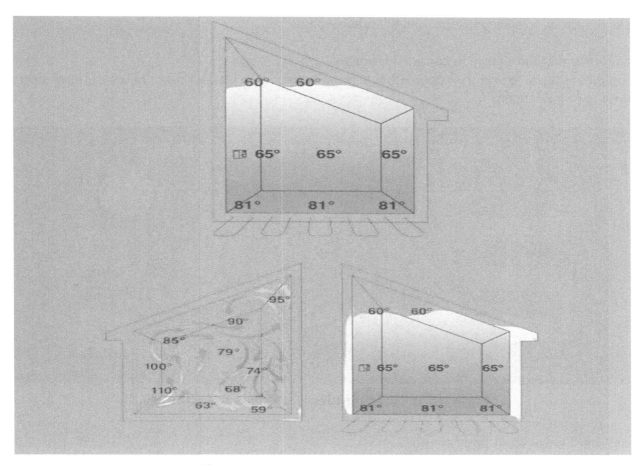

Figure 5.10 Heat Circulating Area

Installation Considerations and Safety Precautions:
Electric heating system installation demands meticulous attention to secure and efficient operation:

Electrical Capacity:
Electric heating systems draw substantial power, necessitating compatibility with the electrical system. Assess the need for electrical panel or circuit upgrades.

Wiring and Connections:
Adept wiring and connections are indispensable to avert electrical hazards and guarantee dependable operation. Engaging a licensed electrician for installation is recommended.

Compliance with Building Codes:
Adherence to local electrical and building codes is imperative for electric heating system compliance. Familiarize oneself with pertinent requirements and regulations in your area.

Safety Measures:
Incorporate apt safety features, such as circuit breakers, ground fault circuit interrupters (GFCIs), and smoke detectors, to safeguard the system and occupants.

Operation and Maintenance Recommendations:
To uphold electric heating system efficiency and efficacy, consider the following operation and maintenance guidelines:

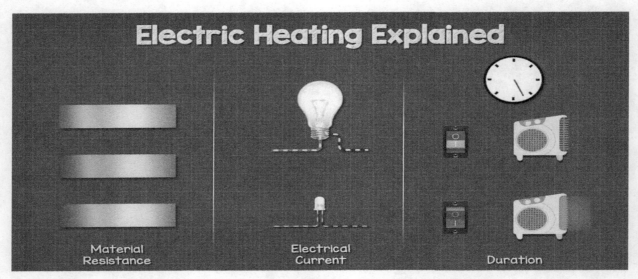

Figure 5.11 Heating Electric Wires Resistance

Thermostat Settings and Programming:
Employ programmable thermostats for temperature control based on occupancy patterns. Program lower temperatures during unoccupied periods for energy conservation sans compromising comfort.

Cleaning and Inspecting Electric Heaters:
Regularly clean electric heater surfaces to eliminate dust and debris. Inspect for signs of damage, like frayed wires or loose connections, and address them promptly. Ensure unobstructed heaters, free from airflow impediments.

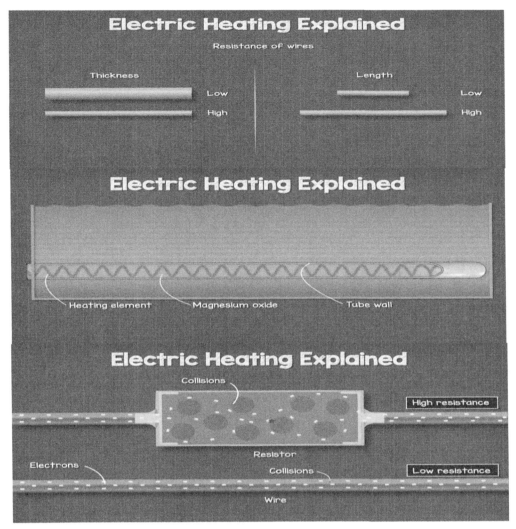

Figure 5.12 Heating Electric Wires Thickness

Troubleshooting Common Issues:
Familiarize yourself with commonplace issues, e.g., thermostat malfunctions, tripped breakers, or heating element failures. Simple troubleshooting measures, such as breaker resets or thermostat replacements, often resolve minor quandaries.

Energy Efficiency Enhancement Strategies:
Implement energy-saving practices, like programmable thermostat use, enhanced insulation, and air leak sealing, to optimize electric heating system energy efficiency. Additionally, consider integrating electric heating systems with renewable energy sources, e.g., solar panels, to curtail environmental impact.
Electric heating systems exude simplicity, versatility, and effective heating solutions. By comprehending different types, installation requisites, and maintenance exigencies, individuals can make enlightened decisions when selecting and utilizing electric heating systems to cater to their heating requirements.

Book 6

HVAC System Design and Energy Efficiency

Load Calculation and Design Considerations

Load calculation is a fundamental step in HVAC system design that determines the heating and cooling requirements of a space. By accurately assessing the load, HVAC professionals can design systems that provide optimal comfort and energy efficiency. In this section, we will explore the importance of load calculation, factors affecting load calculation, calculation methods, and design considerations for different building types.

Figure 6.1 Understanding a Cold Room

Importance of Load Calculation

Load calculation is the process of determining the amount of heating or cooling needed to maintain a comfortable indoor environment. It considers factors such as the size of the space, insulation levels, number of occupants, equipment heat gain, and climate conditions. Proper load calculation ensures that the HVAC system is correctly sized, preventing energy waste, insufficient heating or cooling, and discomfort.

Accurate load calculation offers the following benefits:

Right-sized HVAC System: By determining the exact heating and cooling requirements, load calculation helps in selecting an appropriately sized HVAC system. Oversized systems lead to short cycling, energy waste, and poor humidity control, while undersized systems struggle to meet the desired temperature, resulting in discomfort.

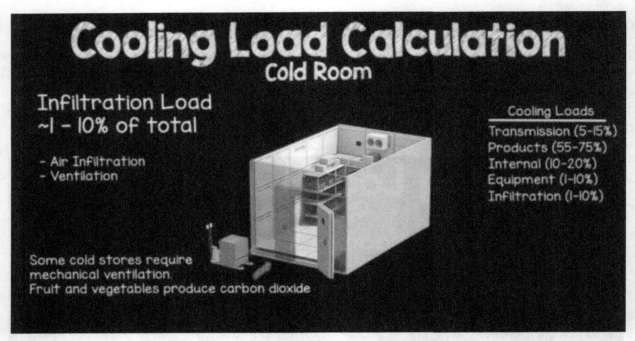

Figure 6.2 Cold Room Infiltration Load

Energy Efficiency: A properly sized HVAC system operates efficiently, reducing energy consumption and utility costs. It avoids unnecessary cycling, maintains stable indoor temperatures, and optimizes the system's performance.

Comfort and Air Quality: Load calculation ensures that the HVAC system can adequately meet the thermal demands of the space, resulting in consistent comfort levels. Proper ventilation and air circulation can also be accounted for, improving indoor air quality.

Factors Affecting Load Calculation
Several factors influence load calculation in HVAC system design. It's essential to consider these factors to accurately assess the heating and cooling requirements of a space. Some key factors include:

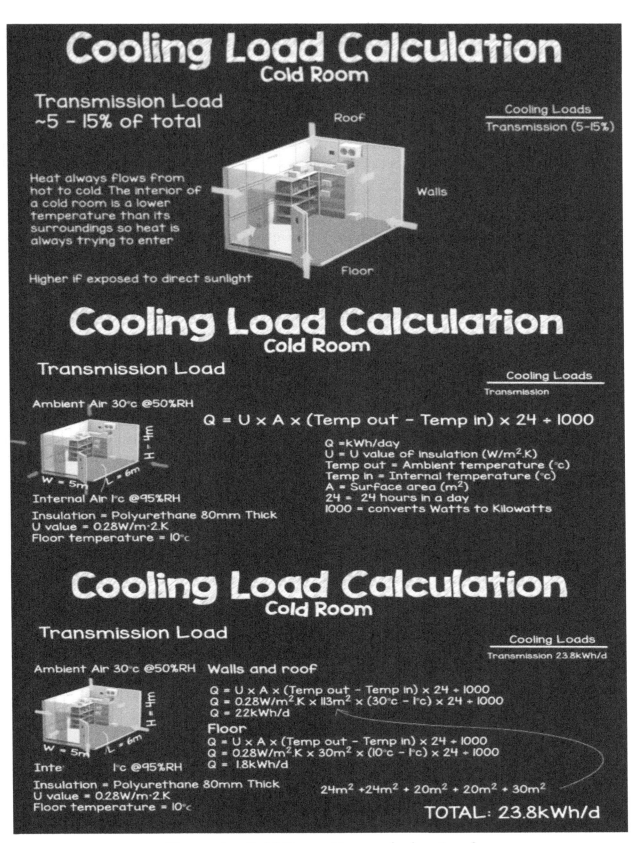

Figure 6.3 Cold Room Transmission Load

Climate: The climate conditions of the region impact the heating and cooling loads. Variables such as outdoor temperature, humidity levels, and solar radiation play a crucial role in determining the load.

Building Envelope: The construction and insulation levels of the building envelope affect heat gain and loss. Factors such as wall construction, insulation materials, windows, doors, and roof design impact the load calculation.

Internal Heat Gain: Internal heat sources, such as lighting fixtures, appliances, and occupants, contribute to the total load. The number of occupants, their activity levels, and the heat generated by equipment should be accounted for.

Ventilation Requirements: Proper ventilation is essential for indoor air quality. Ventilation load considers the fresh air requirements based on the occupancy and the level of outdoor air exchange necessary for maintaining a healthy environment.

Calculation Methods

Various methods are used for load calculation, ranging from manual calculations to sophisticated software programs. Here are some commonly used methods:

Heat Gain/Loss Calculation: This method involves calculating the heat gained or lost through the building envelope based on factors such as wall area, U-value, solar heat gain coefficient, and infiltration rates.

Peak Load Calculation: Peak load calculation determines the maximum heating or cooling load required at a specific time, accounting for various factors like outdoor temperature, occupancy, equipment usage, and solar radiation.

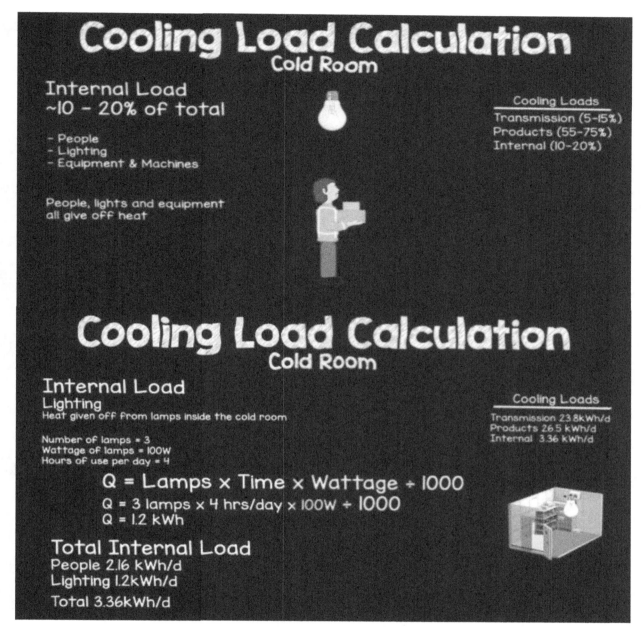

Figure 6.4 Cold Room Internal Loads

Diversity Factors: Diversity factors consider the probability that all heating or cooling loads will occur simultaneously. By applying appropriate diversity factors, the total load can be reduced, preventing oversizing of the HVAC system.

Design Considerations for Different Building Types
Load calculation and design considerations may vary depending on the type of building. Here are some key design considerations for different building types:

113

Cooling Load Calculation
Cold Room

Equipment Load
Defrost - Electrical defrost
Heat given off by the heating element

Defrost element power 1.2kW
Defrost time 30mins
Defrost cycles 3
Defrost efficiency 30%

$$Q = Power \times Time \times Cycles \times efficiency$$

Q = kWh/d
Power = Rating of heating element (kW)
Time = Defrost run time (hours)
Cycles = How many daily cycles
Efficiency = % of heat dissipated into cold room

Cooling Load Calculation
Cold Room

Equipment Load
Fan motors
Heat given off by the fan motors

Number of fans = 3
Wattage of fans = 200W
Hours of use per day = 14

$$Q = Fans \times Time \times Wattage \div 1000$$

Q = kWh/day
Fans = Number of fans
Time = daily run hours (hours)
Wattage = (Watts)

1000 = Conversion Watts to kW

Figure 6.5 Cold Room Equipments Loads

Residential Buildings: Consider the number of bedrooms, living spaces, kitchen requirements, and occupant comfort preferences. Zoning and duct layout should be planned to provide individual temperature control.

Commercial Buildings: Determine the load based on the type of commercial space, such as offices, retail stores, or restaurants. Consider factors like occupancy, equipment heat gain, lighting, and ventilation requirements. Zoning and air distribution must be designed for efficient operation and occupant comfort.

Industrial Buildings: Load calculation for industrial buildings involves analyzing heat gain from machinery, process equipment, and the occupancy factor. Adequate ventilation and air quality considerations should be accounted for.

Institutional Buildings: Institutions like schools, hospitals, and universities have unique load calculation requirements. Factors like occupancy, special equipment, ventilation demands, and critical areas (e.g., operating rooms) must be considered.

By understanding load calculation principles and considering design considerations for different building types, HVAC professionals can create efficient and effective systems that meet the specific heating and cooling needs of various spaces. Accurate load calculation ensures comfort, energy efficiency, and optimal system performance.

Duct Design and Airflow Optimization

Duct design and airflow optimization are pivotal aspects in the realm of HVAC system design, wielding direct influence over efficiency and performance in heating, ventilation, and air conditioning systems. A well-structured ductwork configuration guarantees seamless airflow dispersion, curtails energy losses, and maximizes comfort levels. This discourse delves into the gravity of duct design, diverse duct system types, sizing methodologies, airflow balancing, and optimization techniques.

Significance of Duct Design:
Duct design assumes a pivotal role in determining HVAC system performance, chiefly dictating air distribution efficacy, thus engendering even temperatures and adept ventilation. A meticulously designed duct system engenders an array of advantages:

Efficient Airflow: Properly sized and skillfully designed ductwork facilitates accurate air distribution across each room or zone in the structure, thereby diminishing resistance and pressure drops, culminating in optimal HVAC system operation.

Energy Efficiency: Duct design profoundly influences HVAC system energy efficiency, culminating in minimized air leakage, limited heat gain or loss, and optimized airflow, ultimately resulting in reduced utility expenses.

Comfort and Indoor Air Quality: Apropos airflow distribution fosters uniform temperatures and ventilation, culminating in enhanced comfort and indoor air quality. Well-balanced airflow precludes thermal discrepancies and wards off stagnant air.

Diverse Duct System Types:
HVAC installations incorporate a gamut of duct systems, each bearing distinct advantages and applications. Prominent duct system types include:

Round Ducts: Round ducts manifest as efficacious conduits for air travel, adeptly suited for extended, linear runs. Exhibiting lower resistance and reduced air leakage vis-à-vis other duct shapes.

Rectangular Ducts: Rectangular ducts pervade residential and commercial applications, being facilely installed in compact spaces and yielding a cost-effective alternative for specific installations vis-à-vis round ducts.

Flexible Ducts: Exuding versatility and facile maneuverability, flexible ducts prove suitable for space-constrained installations or irregular layouts. Frequently deployed for connecting supply and return air outlets to main ducts.

Duct Sizing and Layout:
Adequate duct sizing is pivotal to uphold commendable airflow and minimize pressure drops. Duct sizing hinges upon factors such as airflow volume, velocity, and the resistance of the duct material. Undersized ducts may yield reduced airflow, while oversized ducts could occasion excessive noise and inefficient operation.

Critical considerations for duct sizing and layout encompass:

Calculating Airflow Requirements: Assess the requisite airflow volume via load calculations, desideratum for temperature differentials, and ventilation requirements, culminating in ascertaining appropriate duct size.

Friction Loss and Pressure Drops: Account for friction losses and pressure drops stemming from airflow resistance within the duct system. Utilize duct design software or adhere to industry guidelines for calculating suitable duct dimensions.

Duct Material and Insulation: Opt for duct materials evincing low resistance and insulate ducts in unconditioned areas to curtail heat gain or loss. Insulation safeguards the desired air temperature during duct traversal.

Airflow Balancing and Zoning:
Airflow balancing encompasses calibrating airflow rates across disparate branches or zones within the HVAC system to ensure judicious distribution. Balancing takes cognizance of discrepancies in heating and cooling loads, room dimensions, and occupant preferences. Conversely, zoning delimits spaces into discrete regions equipped with autonomous temperature control, thus engendering superior energy efficiency and customized comfort.

Key considerations for airflow balancing and zoning incorporate:

Balancing Dampers: Integrate dampers within diverse branches of the duct system to regulate airflow. Manipulating these dampers ensures airflow balance and commensurate distribution to each area.

Zoning Controls: Employ zoning controls and motorized dampers to partition the space into autonomous zones, each governed by distinct temperature control mechanisms. This fosters tailored comfort and energy preservation via directed conditioning of requisite areas.

Room-by-Room Analysis: Scrutinize the heating and cooling requisites of individual rooms to ascertain fitting airflow rates. Larger rooms or spaces laden with substantial heat loads may necessitate augmented airflow, whereas more confined spaces may warrant diminished airflow.

Airflow Optimization Techniques:
Optimizing airflow within the duct system contributes to energy efficiency and comfort. Apt airflow mitigates burden on the HVAC equipment, ensures consistent temperature dissemination, and heightens indoor air quality. Noteworthy airflow optimization techniques include:

Duct Sealing: Diligently seal duct joints and connections to minimize air leakage. Air leaks result in prodigious energy losses and compromised system performance. Preside over approved sealing materials and techniques to forestall leaks.

Duct Insulation: Insulate ductwork within unconditioned areas to fend off heat gain or loss. Insulation mitigates temperature fluctuations within the ducts and preserves the desired air temperature during distribution.

Airflow Testing and Balancing: Conduct airflow testing to gauge and verify airflow rates across disparate sections of the system. Manipulate dampers and airflow volumes as deemed necessary to attain desired balance and ensure equitable airflow distribution.

Airflow Monitoring and Control: Employ airflow monitoring devices and sensors to perpetually oversee and regulate system airflow. This facilitates real-time adjustments and engenders optimal system performance.

Adequate duct design and airflow optimization are vital to engender energy-efficient and comfortable HVAC systems. By scrutinizing duct sizing, layout, airflow balancing, and optimization techniques, HVAC professionals birth efficient systems, characterized by even temperatures, minimized energy waste, and elevated indoor air quality.

Energy-Efficient Equipment Selection

Selecting energy-efficient HVAC equipment is a key aspect of designing an energy-efficient heating, ventilation, and air conditioning system. By choosing equipment with high energy efficiency ratings and incorporating advanced technologies, you can significantly reduce energy consumption, lower utility costs, and minimize environmental impact. In this section, we will explore the importance of energy-efficient equipment, common energy efficiency ratings, considerations for equipment selection, high-efficiency equipment options, and emerging technologies in HVAC equipment.

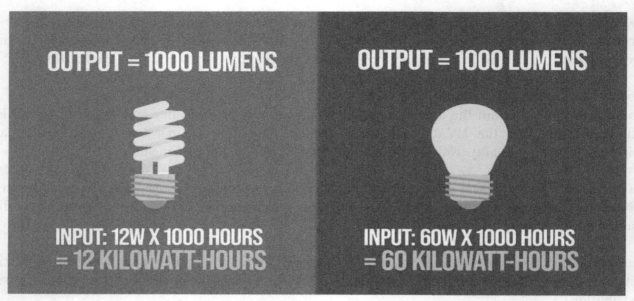

Figure 6.6 Energy-Efficient Equipment

HVAC Equipment Overview

HVAC systems consist of various equipment components, including furnaces, air conditioners, heat pumps, boilers, and more. Each equipment type serves a specific purpose and contributes to the overall performance of the system. When selecting energy-efficient equipment, it's important to consider the following factors:

Energy Efficiency Ratings: Different HVAC equipment types have specific energy efficiency ratings that indicate their performance. These ratings help consumers compare the energy efficiency of different models and make informed choices.

Equipment Size and Capacity: Properly sizing HVAC equipment is essential for optimal energy efficiency. Oversized equipment can lead to short cycling and wasted energy, while undersized equipment may struggle to meet the heating or cooling demands of the space.

Energy Efficiency Ratings and Labels

Energy efficiency ratings and labels provide valuable information about the energy performance of HVAC equipment. Here are some commonly used energy efficiency ratings:

The cooling effectiveness of air conditioners and heat pumps is measured by the seasonal energy efficiency ratio, or SEER. Greater energy efficiency and reduced operating expenses are indicated by a higher SEER rating.

EER (Energy Efficiency Ratio): EER measures the cooling efficiency of air conditioners and heat pumps under specific operating conditions. It provides a snapshot of the equipment's energy performance at a given moment.

AFUE (Annual Fuel Utilization Efficiency): AFUE measures the heating efficiency of furnaces and boilers. It represents the percentage of fuel energy converted into useful heat over an entire heating season. Higher AFUE ratings indicate greater energy efficiency.

Heat pump heating efficiency is gauged by the HSPF (Heating Seasonal Performance Factor). It displays the proportion of heat production to electricity use throughout the course of a heating season. Greater energy efficiency is indicated by higher HSPF ratings.

Energy-efficient equipment often carries energy labels, such as ENERGY STAR, which signifies that the product meets specific energy efficiency guidelines set by the Environmental Protection Agency (EPA) or other regulatory bodies.

Considerations for Equipment Sizing and Selection
When selecting energy-efficient HVAC equipment, several factors should be considered:

Load Calculation Results: Refer to the load calculation results to determine the appropriate equipment size and capacity for heating and cooling requirements. Right-sizing the equipment ensures optimal energy efficiency and performance.

Energy Efficiency Ratings: Compare the energy efficiency ratings of different equipment models. Look for equipment with higher SEER, EER, AFUE, or HSPF ratings to ensure better energy performance.

Manufacturer's Reputation: Consider equipment from reputable manufacturers known for producing high-quality, energy-efficient products. Research customer reviews, industry certifications, and warranty options.

Climate Considerations: Take into account the specific climate conditions in the area where the equipment will be installed. Consider whether additional features like humidity control or heat pump defrost cycles are necessary for optimal performance in specific climates.

High-Efficiency Equipment Options and Features
There are several high-efficiency equipment options available that can significantly improve the energy performance of HVAC systems. Some common options include:

Variable-Speed Technology: Variable-speed compressors and motors adjust their speed to match the heating or cooling demand, providing precise temperature control and energy savings.

Two-Stage or Multi-Stage Systems: Two-stage or multi-stage equipment operates at different levels of capacity based on the heating or cooling needs, allowing for greater energy efficiency and improved comfort.

Heat Recovery Ventilation (HRV) Systems: HRV systems recover heat from stale exhaust air and use it to preheat incoming fresh air, reducing the load on the heating system and improving indoor air quality.

Programmable and Smart Thermostats: Programmable and smart thermostats offer advanced scheduling and temperature control options, allowing for energy-saving programming and remote access to adjust settings.

Emerging Technologies in HVAC Equipment
The HVAC industry is continuously evolving, and new technologies are emerging to further enhance energy efficiency. Some emerging technologies in HVAC equipment include:

Geothermal Heat Pumps: Geothermal heat pumps utilize the stable temperature of the earth to provide heating and cooling. They can achieve high energy efficiency and significantly reduce operating costs over the long term.

Solar-Powered HVAC Systems: Solar-powered systems utilize solar energy to generate electricity for HVAC operation, reducing reliance on the grid and lowering energy consumption.

Advanced Controls and Sensors: Advanced control systems and sensors optimize HVAC operation by monitoring occupancy, indoor and outdoor conditions, and adjusting equipment performance accordingly.

Energy Recovery Systems: Energy recovery systems capture and transfer heat or coolness from the exhaust air to the incoming fresh air, reducing the load on the heating or cooling equipment.

By considering energy efficiency ratings, proper sizing, equipment features, and emerging technologies, HVAC professionals can select equipment that maximizes energy efficiency, reduces operating costs, and promotes environmental sustainability. Choosing energy-efficient equipment is a key step towards creating a sustainable and efficient HVAC system.

Building Automation Systems and Controls

Building automation systems (BAS) and controls represent pivotal constituents in optimizing the operation, efficiency, and comfort of heating, ventilation, and air conditioning (HVAC) systems. These systems epitomize centralized monitoring, control, and automation for a diverse array of building functions, encompassing HVAC, lighting, security, and sundry other facets. Within this discourse, we delve into the gravity of building automation systems, the salient components of BAS, the benefits of automation, and considerations pertinent to executing an effective control strategy.

Importance of Building Automation Systems:
Building automation systems yield a myriad of advantages for both commercial and residential structures. These systems furnish centralized control, monitoring, and automation capabilities, thereby streamlining operations, elevating energy efficiency, augmenting occupant comfort, and mitigating maintenance expenses. Key rationales underpinning the importance of building automation systems encompass:

Energy Efficiency: BAS expedites energy consumption optimization through automated adjustment of HVAC settings, lighting schedules, and other building systems predicated on occupancy, external conditions, and pre-established parameters, culminating in energy savings and reduced utility costs.

Comfort and Occupant Satisfaction: Automation affords precision control over temperature, humidity, and ventilation, thus ensuring optimal comfort conditions for occupants. Automation further accords flexibility in customizing settings based on individual preferences or specific building areas.

Operational Efficiency: Centralized monitoring and control expedite facility management undertakings, thereby reducing manual intervention and simplifying maintenance operations. System faults prompt alerts and notifications, thus enabling timely troubleshooting and preventive maintenance.

Sustainability and Environmental Impact: Building automation systems contribute to sustainability endeavors by espousing energy conservation and curtailing greenhouse gas emissions. These systems enable energy-saving stratagems and facilitate integration of renewable energy sources.

Key Components of Building Automation Systems:
Building automation systems integrate multiple components operating in concert to monitor, control, and automate building systems. These components encompass:

Sensors and Actuators: Sensors accumulate data on diverse environmental parameters, including temperature, humidity, occupancy, and air quality. Actuators control equipment operations based on sensor input.

Controllers: Controllers receive data from sensors, undertake processing, and dispatch commands to actuators to effect system adjustments. Functioning as the cerebral locus of the BAS, controllers facilitate communication and decision-making.

A Simplified BAS Architecture Example

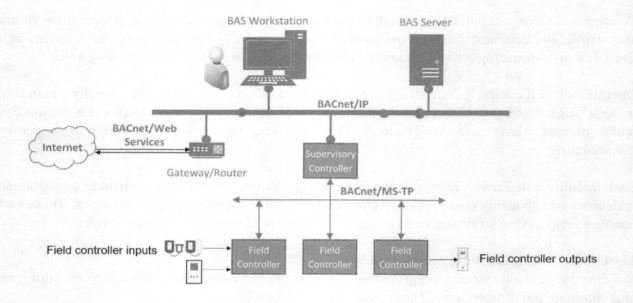

Communications Interface

- For integration with other systems
  - Connect a BAS to other building systems
  - Connect a BAS to the internet
  - Connect a proprietary BAS to an "open" BAS/device or another proprietary BAS/device
- Gateway or Router
- Not an FPOC (Field Point of Connection) device

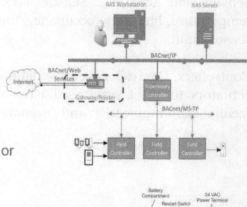

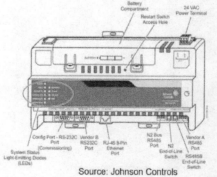

Source: Johnson Controls

Figure 6.7 BAS Controllers

Human-Machine Interface (HMI): HMIs supply user-friendly interfaces for building operators to monitor system performance, adjust settings, and receive notifications. HMIs may encompass graphical displays, dashboards, or mobile applications.

Communication Networks: Communication networks engender information exchange amid diverse BAS components. Wired or wireless protocols, e.g., BACnet, Modbus, or LonWorks, commonly connect sensors, controllers, and ancillary devices.

Integration Software: Integration software facilitates seamless communication and coordination amid diverse building systems, including HVAC, lighting, security, and fire safety. Integration software fosters interoperability and centralized control.

Benefits of Building Automation and Controls:
Deploying building automation systems and controls imparts an array of benefits:

Energy Management: BAS affords precise control over HVAC systems, optimizing energy consumption vis-à-vis occupancy, external conditions, and temporal schedules, hence culminating in appreciable energy savings and diminished utility costs.

Enhanced Comfort and Indoor Air Quality: Automation ensures that temperature, humidity, and ventilation levels are maintained within optimal ranges, thus bestowing occupants with agreeable and salubrious indoor environs.

Fault Detection and Diagnostics: Building automation systems can discern system faults and anomalies, dispatching alerts to prompt maintenance or troubleshooting. Prompt fault detection minimizes downtime and reduces repair expenses.

Demand Response and Load Management: BAS may participate in demand response programs, where energy consumption is adjusted during peak demand periods to buttress grid stability. Load management strategies optimize energy use amid utility pricing fluctuations.

Data Analysis and Reporting: Building automation systems compile and analyze data on energy consumption, system performance, and occupant behavior. Such data facilitates trend identification, evaluation of energy-saving initiatives, and report generation for energy management purposes.

Considerations for Implementing an Effective Control Strategy:
When implementing building automation systems and controls, factors meriting consideration encompass:

System Design and Integration: Proper design and integration of BAS components ensure seamless communication, interoperability, and compatibility with extant building systems, necessitating meticulous planning and coordination among stakeholders.

Setpoint Optimization: Establishing optimal setpoints for temperature, humidity, and ventilation is critical for energy efficiency and occupant comfort. Factors, such as building usage, occupancy patterns, and external conditions, should inform setpoint determination.

Occupant Engagement and Education: Apprise building occupants about the merits of automation and encourage their participation in energy-saving practices. Engaged occupants contribute to energy efficiency by adhering to guidelines and effectively utilizing control features.

Regular Maintenance and Calibration: Building automation systems necessitate periodic maintenance, calibration, and software updates to ensure accurate data collection, reliable performance, and alignment with evolving industry standards.

Building automation systems and controls wield formidable potential for maximizing energy efficiency, heightening occupant comfort, and optimizing building operations. By leveraging automation technology and implementing effective control strategies, HVAC professionals can erect smarter, more sustainable buildings that cater to occupants' needs while minimizing environmental impact.

Energy Efficiency Strategies and Sustainability

Energy efficiency and sustainability are essential considerations in designing and operating heating, ventilation, and air conditioning (HVAC) systems. By implementing energy efficiency strategies and adopting sustainable practices, HVAC professionals can reduce energy consumption, lower greenhouse gas emissions, and contribute to a more environmentally friendly future. In this section, we will explore key energy efficiency strategies, sustainable HVAC practices, and the benefits of prioritizing sustainability in HVAC systems.

Energy Efficiency Strategies
Energy efficiency strategies focus on optimizing HVAC system performance to minimize energy consumption without compromising comfort. Here are some key strategies to consider:

Proper System Sizing: Ensure HVAC equipment is properly sized according to building load calculations. Oversized or undersized equipment can result in energy waste, reduced efficiency, and increased operating costs.

High-Efficiency Equipment: Select HVAC equipment with high energy efficiency ratings, such as ENERGY STAR certified models. These units utilize advanced technologies and design features to maximize energy performance.

Zoning and Controls: Implement zoning systems and advanced controls to tailor heating and cooling based on occupancy and specific area requirements. This allows for customized comfort and energy savings by directing conditioned air where it is needed most.

Regular Maintenance: Schedule regular maintenance to keep HVAC systems in optimal condition. Clean or replace air filters, inspect and clean coils, and ensure proper refrigerant levels. Well-maintained systems operate more efficiently and have a longer lifespan.

Airflow Optimization: Optimize duct design, seal ductwork, and balance airflow to minimize air leakage and ensure proper distribution of conditioned air. This improves system efficiency, reduces energy waste, and enhances comfort.

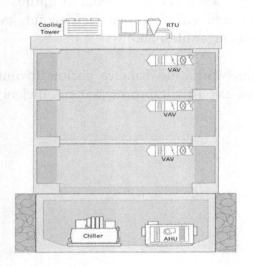

A typical commercial building with HVAC equipment

- Chiller
- Air handling unit
- Variable-Air-Volume (VAV) terminal unit
- Cooling tower
- Rooftop Unit (RTU)
- Fans, pumps, fin tube radiators, etc. (not shown)

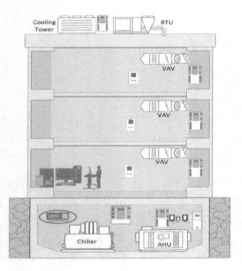

HVAC controls components

- Field controller
- Field controller inputs
  - Thermostat and CT
- Field controller outputs
  - VFD, VAV dampers, etc.
- Supervisory controller
- Operator workstation
- Server
- Network communication interface

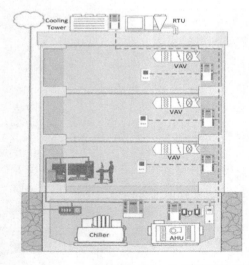

BAS network – 3-tier system architecture

- Enterprise IT network (high speed) _____
- Building control network (BCN, high speed) _____
- Field control network (FCN, low speed) _ _ _ _ _ _

Figure 6.8 HVAC House Building Network

126

Programmable and Smart Thermostats: Install programmable or smart thermostats that allow for automated temperature adjustments based on occupancy patterns and time schedules. This helps save energy by reducing unnecessary heating or cooling when spaces are unoccupied.

Energy Recovery Systems: Incorporate energy recovery systems, such as heat exchangers, to capture and reuse waste heat or coolness from exhaust air. These systems help reduce energy demand and improve overall efficiency.

Sustainable HVAC Practices
In addition to energy efficiency, adopting sustainable HVAC practices further contributes to environmental stewardship. Here are some sustainable practices to consider:
Renewable Energy Integration: Explore the integration of renewable energy sources, such as solar panels or geothermal heat pumps, to power HVAC systems. Renewable energy reduces reliance on fossil fuels and lowers greenhouse gas emissions.

Aim for green building certifications that recognize sustainable construction techniques, such as LEED (Leadership in Energy and Environmental Design). These accreditations support indoor environmental quality, water conservation, and energy efficiency.

Indoor Air Quality: Implement strategies to maintain good indoor air quality, such as using high-efficiency air filters, proper ventilation, and regular maintenance. Clean indoor air enhances occupant health and productivity.

Water Conservation: Consider water-efficient HVAC technologies, such as water-cooled chillers or condensing boilers, and implement water management practices to reduce water consumption and promote sustainability.

Lifecycle Assessment: Conduct lifecycle assessments to evaluate the environmental impact of HVAC systems from manufacturing to disposal. Consider materials, energy use, and waste management practices to identify opportunities for improvement.

Benefits of Prioritizing Sustainability
Prioritizing sustainability in HVAC systems offers several benefits:

Energy Cost Savings: Energy-efficient and sustainable practices lead to reduced energy consumption, resulting in lower utility bills and operational costs.

Environmental Impact: Sustainable HVAC systems contribute to a greener environment by reducing greenhouse gas emissions, minimizing resource depletion, and promoting renewable energy usage.

Improved Indoor Comfort: Energy-efficient systems with proper airflow, temperature control, and ventilation enhance occupant comfort and well-being.
Enhanced Building Value: Buildings with sustainable HVAC systems often have higher market value and appeal to environmentally conscious tenants or buyers.

Regulatory Compliance: By adopting sustainable practices, building owners and operators can comply with energy efficiency regulations and environmental standards set by local authorities.

By implementing energy efficiency strategies and sustainable HVAC practices, professionals can create more efficient, eco-friendly systems that provide optimal comfort while minimizing environmental impact. Embracing sustainability not only benefits building owners and occupants but also contributes to a more sustainable future for generations to come.

References

-What is HVAC?
https://www.trane.com/residential/en/resources/glossary/what-is-hvac/
-Heating, ventilation, and air conditioning
https://en.wikipedia.org/wiki/Heating,_ventilation,_and_air_conditioning
-Types of HVAC Systems
https://www.intechopen.com/chapters/62059
-HVAC Installation: Learn The Process In 6 Steps
https://www.forbes.com/home-improvement/hvac/hvac-installation/
-VENTS - manufacture of ventilation and air conditioning systems
https://ventilation-system.com/
-Whole-House Ventilation
https://www.energy.gov/energysaver/whole-house-ventilation
-Heat Recovery Ventilation
https://www.andrianos.gr/en/products/ventilation-systems-with-heat-recovery
-Air conditioning
https://en.wikipedia.org/wiki/Air_conditioning
-Heating technologies | EHI
https://ehi.eu/heating-technologies/
-What Is The Future Of Technology And Home Heating?
https://www.uktech.news/what-is-the-future-of-technology-and-home-heating
-What is Hydronic Heating?
https://www.hydronic.com.au/what-is-hydronic-heating/
-Tips for energy-efficient HVAC design
https://www.essentracomponents.com/en-gb/news/industries/hvac/how-to-design-an-energy-efficient-hvac
-HVAC Load Calculator - Manual J Calculation | ServiceTitan
https://www.servicetitan.com/tools/hvac-load-calculator#:~:text=HVAC%20Load%20Calculation%20Example,12%20windows%20x%201%2C000%20%3D%2012%2C000
-The Basic Principles of Duct Design, Part 1
https://www.energyvanguard.com/blog/basic-principles-duct-design/
-Building Automation System Easy Guide to Learning 101
https://highperformancehvac.com/building-automation-systems-hvac-control/
-Sustainable HVAC systems in commercial construction
https://www.construction21.org/articles/h/sustainable-hvac-systems-in-commercial-construction-balancing-comfort-and-energy-efficiency.html
-How the HVAC Industry is Evolving for Sustainability - Grainger
https://www.grainger.com/know-how/equipment-information/kh-how-the-hvac-industry-is-evolving-for-sustainability
-Top 8 sustainable HVAC solutions
https://www.barbourproductsearch.info/top-8-sustainable-hvac-solutions-blog000441.html